DARE TO RE...

TREASURES OF DARKNESS

Gill Gifford

Website: gillcuttingedge.org
Email: gillcuttingedge2020@gmail.com

2020

First Edition

Published and Printed by

Leiston Press

Masterlord Industrial Estate

Leiston

Suffolk

IP16 4JD

Telephone Number: 01728 833003

Email: glenn@leistonpress.com

ISBN 978-1-911311-66-9

ACKNOWLEDGEMENTS

This book is dedicated first and foremost to my Beloved Saviour Jesus Christ. I never want to forget or take for granted all He has done for me at the Cross. I am forever grateful that He delivered me out of the realm of darkness and brought me into His wonderful light. My desire is to know Him more and experience the power flowing out of His resurrection, share His sufferings and be transformed into His likeness....... Jesus you are my God and my Beloved and I love you with all my heart!

Next I want to appreciate my dear husband Skippy for his patience, love and support he has given me over many years. We have had a very special time during this Lockdown period, and I have enjoyed reading the Word aloud to him every day. It blesses me to hear Skippy worshipping as he sits on the terrace!

My special thanks go to all my very precious family who honour us. I love you all....so gifted and unique with SO many different qualities! Especially I want to thank my lovely, talented and very busy daughter, Meryl, who once again has made time to proof-read this latest book.

So many asked when I was going to write another book. I never thought it would happen... but here it is!! To you my extended family, daughters and sons in the Lord, you are my dearest friends and all who have supported the ministry in hospitality, finance, prayer and love over many years... An ENORMOUS THANK YOU!! Without you I would never have survived these last twenty years, let alone been able to write five books... you all have a very special place engraved in my heart! Thank you for being there for me in those stretchy times!

Finally, to you... yes, the ones who will buy this book... thank you for "sowing" into the ministry. I may not know you or even get to know you, but you are really precious beyond price and although unseen by me... your Heavenly Father sees and loves you! I pray that this book will bring the anointing of the Holy Spirit into your lives in a very real and positive way and inspire you to press towards your own personal destiny long after I go from this world!

So, enjoy treasure hunting with the Lord... it's a great adventure!

DARE to RECEIVE the TREASURES of DARKNESS!

CONTENTS

FOREWORD

1.
Wynne Goss D.div., D.S.M.: Apostle, International Speaker.
www.wynnegoss.com

When the Messenger of the Lord communicates at the divinely inspired Moment, then the Message they are given to share imparts to the reader God's grace and faith ability to step into it.

This book, **Dare To Receive the Treasures of Darkness**, written and released by Gill, has these three ingredients. The Messenger and the Message contained in these pages, are in alignment with each other. You will not read Gill's theories about this subject, but honest, personal, real experience on every page to confirm she has walked this road with Holy Spirit for many years and it is all etched indelibly into her heart and lifestyle.

You will discover, as you read this book, the Moment of its publication and release is also divinely appointed. The alignment of all three assures that this Message comes to you at Holy Spirit's appointed time to bring it to pass in your life. This is why this book will be so explosive and life changing for everyone who reads it, receiving it as Father's free gift of grace for their life.

So, what will you get when you read this book?

As I have already stated, you will get reality, honesty and humility. I have known Gill for almost 40 years now, and as I read this book it was as if she was right here in the room with me, sharing it all. It is written just as she speaks in person, unfolding and sharing even her weaknesses and doubts, followed by how Father's grace moved her into miraculous moments. She is not afraid to be real with you. That is why you can trust her to speak into your life.

What else will you get when reading this book?

You will sense, just like me when I read this book, our Father's loving words that lift you. Like a pair of arms, His love will wrap around your heart to comfort and encourage you to believe and trust in His ability, more than your own, because of His unfailing love towards you. Oh, how many healing moments like this I personally received as I read this book.

Finally, I assure you that by the end of reading **Dare To Receive the Treasures of Darkness**, you will discover that every book of the Bible carries the understanding that Father turns every situation that looks incredibly dark, or confusing, into the dawning of our brightest moment, just as He did for Abraham, David, Job and Paul. He has not changed. He will do for you the same in every situation you face and go through, trusting Him to be your eternal Saviour, Deliverer, Provider and Protector.

Do not waste this divinely inspired Moment. Read this book and let Holy Spirit transform your life by revealing just who Jesus Christ really is in you and who you really are in Him. See everything with new perspective and you will release the Victor from within you, instead of feeling like you are the Victim.

Father created and destined you for greatness. He fashioned you to rule and reign over every circumstance in life, not live downtrodden by even one of them. Page by page, Gill's teaching and personal testimonies will show you how you can **Dare to Receive the Treasures of Darkness** in every moment of life and experience the same miraculous outcomes that she personally shares with you in this book. The emphasis of the message contained within her and this book is not at all about her own great ability or faith, but the ability and loving faithfulness of our Father in Heaven.

I am honoured and delighted to unreservedly recommend both Gill Gifford, the Messenger, and this Message, **Dare to Receive the Treasures of Darkness,** to you at this divinely appointed Moment.

2.
Bern & Maureen Howe: Over-seeing the Cutting Edge Ministry, Pastors, Pioneers, Church Planters, Counsellors, Prayer Warriors & friends to many in the Body of Christ

This is certainly Gilly's best book so far yet. Once again it is beautifully and sensitively written, an excellent book of how to live our lives after all the down times and turn them into stepping-stones to go on to achieve great things. This book will show you it is possible to receive treasures from our darkest hours. You will be encouraged as you read and learn most valuable lessons to press on into the rest of your life. Read it... digest it... live it yourself and you will store up treasures in Heaven!

3.
Rev. John Hindmarsh and Angie Hindmarsh: Bible Teachers and dear friends

Gill is unstoppable! Unstoppable in her love and commitment to the Lord Jesus, the Word of God, in keeping in step with the Holy Spirit, and in genuine love for all people.

It's no wonder, then, that 'Dare to Receive the Treasures of Darkness' is the theme of Gill's latest book – a book to lift the spirits and encourage us into light and life, no matter how dark the current situation is in which we find ourselves.

Dive into this book as a whole or in bite-size pieces for meditation, inspiration, education, encouragement, wisdom for life and that all important action. Thank you, Gill.

4.
Sarah Watkins: Healing Evangelist www.healing2thenaitons.co.uk

Another fantastic and timely book written by Gill Gifford, that will challenge you, pushing you forward into all that God has for you in the days ahead.

You will hear Gill's passion and love emanating from every page inspiring and encouraging you to go forward in trusting the Lord.

There is a very clear and fantastic balance of clear biblical teaching using many books and accounts from the Bible, plus many true-life experiences and testimonies. All of these are full of the Holy Spirit and will serve to build a foundation of faith and expectancy within you for your next season.

This book will bring clarity and increase your peace and trust in God as you discover Treasures hidden in Darkness for your life too!

Open your heart and be prepared to be challenged and changed forever by the Word and power of God.

5.
Jonathan Conrathe: Founder and Director Mission 24

In "Dare to receive the Treasures of darkness", Gill exhorts us that "darkness is God's opportunity", that He is working in every situation of our lives, and if we reach out to Him, hear His Word, believe and respond, He will bring transformation, victory, and fruitfulness out of even the most challenging of situations, conforming us to the glorious image of His Son in the process! Taking us on a fabulous journey through the pages and heroes of Scripture, Gill brilliantly reminds us that when we respond in faith to God rather than reacting in fear to circumstances, our Father births miracles out of mysteries, breakthroughs out of burdens, and new seasons out of old... the Treasures of Darkness!

Introducing Gill Gifford and the Cutting Edge

Gill had a dramatic Salvation experience on Boxing Day 1979, when she died and went to heaven and God sent her back to do the works He had prepared for her to do. Subsequently she went, with her husband Skippy, to Bible School Training under the excellent supervision of Colin Urquhart and the late Bob Gordon. Since 1984 Gill has, along with her husband, been in leadership in different places in UK and they spent 7 years leading an English Church in Mallorca in Spain, where they still live and travel from. Gill has been married to Skippy for 45years; they have two children and five grandchildren.

Cutting Edge Ministries was born as a result of much encouragement from doing a number of Conferences. For ten years, Gill regularly led Seminars for Rachel Hickson across the UK and in Northern Ireland. For the last 18 years, Gill has been travelling to different countries as an Inspirational Preacher doing Conferences and visiting Churches. Then, 16 years ago, The Holy Spirit urged Gill to host her own Cutting Edge Conferences... one in the South at Windmill Farm Conference Centre and one in the North at Abbot Hall in Grange-over-Sands. Five years ago, Gill handed over these Conferences to Healing Evangelist Sarah Watkins. There is now one main Conference... "Healing to the Nations" ... held each year at the Telford International Centre in the Midlands.

The Regional "Without Limits" Day Conferences for men and women are still being held as Inspirational Days of Encouragement, Ministry and Testimony. This is fulfilling the Lord's Commission to... Believe in, Encourage, Disciple and Release the Body of Christ into their ministry. Gill, still at 81 years, has a team of dedicated men and women who support and enable her to do all these things!

Gill is forever grateful to Apostle Dr Wynne Goss for his spiritual cover over many previous years. Now, in these later days, Gill is blessed with the covering of Bern and Maureen Howe, Pastors and Pioneers to so many in the Body of Christ. Their friendship, prayer, wise counselling and standing alongside both Gill and Skippy in this different season is and has been invaluable!

Why Cutting Edge? Because so often lives have been wounded, damaged and hurt by the cutting edge of people's words, past traumatic situations; while others have been pierced, crushed or even stabbed by the circumstances of life. In fact, everyone has been on the cutting edge at certain times! But the Good News is that Jesus came to heal the broken-hearted, to proclaim liberty to the physical and spiritual captives and the opening of the prisons and the eyes of those who are blind and to:

PROCLAIM... THIS IS THE YEAR OF HIS POWER AND FAVOUR!

The Sailing Boat represents the TRUE CUTTING EDGE of the Spirit-filled life of freedom, excitement, progress, purpose and leaning into God in total dependency on Him. It means cutting the moorings that hold us back, launching out into all that God has for us and allowing the Holy Spirit to take us out on the great swelling tide of His plans and purposes. The Cutting Edge encourages people to leave behind the safe, smooth waters of the harbour, and move out into the great unfathomable riches of Christ to fulfil their destiny! It means to let down your spiritual nets into deep waters and also to soar above and beyond the circumstances of life.

In the dark difficult seasons, there are treasures to be experienced. Again and again, you will receive the Glorious Empowering of the Beautiful Holy Spirit to take you further in these challenging times we live in and make a difference wherever you go!

DARE to RECEIVE the TREASURES of DARKNESS

"DARE to RECEIVE the TREASURES of DARKNESS"

By

Gill Gifford

INTRODUCTION

Isaiah 45:3... "I will give you the treasures of darkness and hidden riches of secret places that you may know that it is I the Lord, the God of Israel, Who calls you by name."

When I wrote my last book... "Dare to Experience the Cross" ... I honestly never expected the Lord to ask me to write another book! I know I have said the same thing after finishing each of the books!! After all, I am 81 years old and my computer skills, that I had, are rusty to say the least!! But here I am, as many others are, in "Lockdown" here in Mallorca due to the Pandemic of Corona Virus. Skippy and I have been enjoying my reading the Bible aloud to him each day... he cannot read now as he has degenerative damage in his left retina and a hole in the right retina. We have completed the whole of the Bible together and have begun reading again all of the New Testament... What a joy it has been!! It was as I was reading the Big Picture at the beginning of Genesis that the Holy Spirit really quickened the words to me... This is the BEGINNING of a New Season! So, I asked Him... what is my new beginning?

I need to explain just how I had been feeling at that particular time! As I listened to the News I would just weep and weep... tears that flowed SO much. It was as if my heart was breaking! I knew that the Holy Spirit was doing a very deep work in me, but I didn't know what!! I have learnt that often the Lord doesn't share details of what He is doing until we are ready to respond! I truly examined my heart to see if this was an emotional response to the horrible tragedy of this unseen virus enemy that was attacking the world at this time or; if I was deeply interceding for those in so much grief and pain... or; even if it was God's own heart that He was sharing with me?

I did not know until I listened to a message from T.D. Jakes' daughter, Sarah Jakes Roberts... "Weeping to Walking". She was talking about the need for our passion to have an outlet!!! Suddenly I knew that my passion for Jesus had to have an outlet during this Lockdown season... and the Holy Spirit whispered... Yes! Gill you need to write another book about **"The Treasures in the Darkness"**!

The more I thought about it, the more I realized that I had been actually preaching from this text in Isaiah for the last six months, the more I have shared, the more revelation that the Spirit has opened up to me as the Holy Spirit walked me personally through the Bible! In fact, I was confronted with this when a Pastor asked me recently to share a short word for his Church family to encourage them. I got carried away with **"The Treasures of Darkness"** at this particularly difficult time and it turned out to be far too long to send by the Internet... it was just flowing out of me as a river from deep inside me! So, I had to re-do a shorter message... but deep inside me I felt I was stifling the Spirit! THEN... I heard that word! **"Your passion must have an outlet!"**

Suddenly I knew that the Spirit was speaking clearly to me... however difficult and challenging I might find it... I had to write another book during this Lockdown season here at home in Mallorca!!! Previously, several people had repeatedly asked me when the next book would be on sale. To which I always said, "No! Much too difficult now Skippy has been diagnosed with Alzheimer's and Dementia."

BUT GOD had other plans!!! So here I am making a start... it's another adventure with my beautiful Friend and Helper, the Holy Spirit! Yes! I am excited; yet trembling in His Presence... Lots of questions! ... Can I do it? Will He really enable me to open **"The Treasures of Darkness"** to you? Will I be able to release these amazing treasures so that they will bless and build up the Body of Christ? I truly am completely dependent on His ability and His inspiration, knowing that if God wants me to do this, He will be my Enabler.

This Scripture in Isaiah 45:3... **"I will give you Treasures of Darkness and hidden riches of secret places"** ... This is a real personal promise from the Word of God. The Bible says in... 2 Corinthians 1:20 "ALL His promises are "Yes" and "Amen" in Christ Jesus to the Glory of God." I just happen to believe that what God writes in His Word is Truth and He means every word that is written... whether I understand it or not, whether I experience it or not! It is His God-breathed Scripture!

So, my beloved ones... we are living in such unprecedented times, never in any of our wildest dreams or imaginations could we have foreseen such a scenario in our world as we are living in right now. There may be the terrible facts around us right now, **YET.... God's TRUTH stands firm beyond all circumstances and He is forever faithful** to His nature of eternal goodness and His supernatural power is greater than everything we see or hear about in our natural realm.

As Believers, the Bible says: Colossians 1:13 "The Father has delivered and drawn us to Himself out of the control and dominion of darkness and has transferred us into the Kingdom of the Son of His love." As Born-Again children of the Most High God, we have been delivered from the kingdom of darkness and brought into the Kingdom of the Beloved Son of God. That is where we are seated and where we see the Truth with complete confidence that the Everlasting Lord God Almighty is the **God who is Love**... He is the Person of Love; **HE IS GOD** who sits above the circle of the earth and His love and power are absolutely OMNIPTOTENT and SUPERNATURAL. God demonstrated that God the Father raised Jesus Christ up from the dead and defeated the last enemy which is death.

He is THE ALL powerful One, the Living God who is the only True God.
The Father Himself has made us His children! Hallelujah!!

SO... you see... there are incredible Treasures available for us during these dark days and the Bible assures us that **God does His best work in the darkness!** Read on and you will experience these Treasures personally, I promise you! This is what has amazed me as I have been preaching this word for at least six months! Could it be that it was more prophetic than I ever realized??? Maybe... I don't know. So that is why I am going to share with you what the Spirit has revealed to me. I really trust that you will see new things and have fresh revelation that will come to you personally so that you can receive the **"Treasures of Darkness"** and that the Spirit Himself will illuminate the Word of God with light and revelation. Jesus said in Luke 21:33... "The sky and the earth will pass away, but my words will not pass away."

The First thing the Lord spoke about to me was that darkness was not a problem to Him! He said: "Gill you have a wrong concept of darkness." OH! OH! OH! I have come to know that if He says something like that... He is right!!! So, my heart and spirit responded... "Teach me Holy Spirit, I am willing to learn... You are the best Teacher anyone could have!"

So, here goes... There really are, I promise you, treasures for each person to search out in His Word and from life's situations! So, my dearest reader, let's go treasure hunting together with the Holy Spirit! Make a decision to receive what the Spirit has for you personally. I can't see who you are, but God knows you and He knew me and you from before the foundation of the world, He knew I would be writing this book even though I had no idea and He knew you would be reading this book! That is SO amazing isn't it? What I do know is that if you are open and soft to the Master's touch, that these **"Treasures of Darkness"** will bring The Lord's special blessings into your life and, maybe, make sense of this seemingly senseless time we are living in.

"DARE to RECEIVE the TREASURES of DARKNESS"

Chapter 1.

WHAT IS DARKNESS?

–

The first thing that the Holy Spirit said to me was to explore and research about darkness... then The Holy Spirit said He would take me for a walk through the Word of God and highlight new things to me! He said I would understand better, then, as to how I could **"Receive the Treasures of Darkness"** in my own life experiences! How wonderful is that?!!! SO...

The Webster's Dictionary says: ... Darkness is a VOID and EMPTINESS because it is the ABSENCE of light. It is GLOOM and DIMNESS and BLACKNESS! Because darkness is the absence of light, that is just when the enemy comes slithering in and DISTORTS everything. Yes, the enemy of our souls, Satan, creeps in uninvited and stimulates an illusion that plays with our minds, planting irrational fears and lies that bring emotional responses that affect our bodies, our situations and sometimes all of our lives. Ultimately this produces a STRONGHOLD in our minds of WRONG BELIEF... LIES! Then we believe that darkness is very powerful.

BUT...NO! DARKNESS HAS NO POWER...
IT IS ONLY A DECEPTION!

WOW!!

So now I was beginning to understand a completely new concept of darkness. The Holy Spirit explained that LIGHT can be measured. One or two facts make it SO amazing! Commonly, the speed of Light is measured at: 299,792,458 metres per second... in other words if you could travel round the earth at the speed of light, you could go around the Earth 7.5 times in one second!!!!!

The POWER of LIGHT is PHENOMENAL

Light has been developed into LASER surgery in the most complex ways of compressing light so that power is produced. Those of you who are Physicists will know far more than I do... needless to say I was beginning to realize that LIGHT is far more powerful, and that darkness cannot be measured at all and therefore has NO power! No wonder the Bible says in

John 1:4-5 "In Him was Life and the Life was the Light of men, And the Light shines on in the darkness, for the darkness has never overpowered it, put it out or absorbed it or appropriated it, and is unreceptive to it." In other words:

Darkness runs from LIGHT!!! HALLELUJAH!!!

I am aware that the darkness in our lives is not always a physical darkness... although it can be! So, I asked the Holy Spirit how He saw darkness... I believe it can be anything that troubles us, oppresses us, any difficult times we might be experiencing, any fears or dry period in our lives or crisis that causes pain. It can also be grief at a sudden loss or an illness for you or a loved one. It could be the pressures of work or ministry... it can be spiritual, mental, emotional or physical... so many different reasons to feel as if the darkness is closing in on you. Darkness can also be the absence of something or even someone which leaves a void inside us. The definition The Spirit gave me was: Any place, person or situation that causes us to almost, or completely, lose our vision of Jesus and His amazing love shown at the Cross at Calvary... that is DARKNESS!

Your feelings of darkness may be quite different to mine, but in whatever way it affects you, it is real; and YET....God promises that in the darkness there is an opportunity to experience **"The Treasures of Darkness"** that the Word of God promises you! So, Lord, please will you open our spiritual eyes to see with the eyes of the Holy Spirit so that we don't miss these treasures you have for us!

However, as I am writing this book, I personally felt that I needed the Lord to begin to give me a new perspective and revelation of darkness and that I needed a personal illustration. That is when the Lord reminded me years ago when I was a small child going to bed, I didn't like the dark... so my Mum would give me a little tea-light. But that brought moving shadows and my dressing gown hanging on the back of the bedroom door looked like a faceless nasty person! So, what I would do? I would hide under the bedclothes where I felt safe! Nothing had changed in reality, but the safe place was my hiding place. That was my **"Treasure in that Darkness!"** And do you know what... when the light was put on, or the morning dawned... the dressing gown was just a dressing gown and not a "bogeyman" that could hurt me! The darkness brought an evil illusion and created fears, so I needed to find a treasure... my hiding place was under cover inside my bed clothes... that was my treasure!!! How much more wonderful that we can always find that safe HIDING PLACE in our Heavenly Father's arms... there are always **"Treasures in Darkness"** for us close in His loving embrace!

Just to illustrate in another way, some of you may remember several years ago that there was a mighty outpouring of the Holy Spirit in Toronto... Yes! The Toronto Blessing! You see I SO longed to go there to Canada and receive more of the Holy Spirit, I was SO hungry for everything that God wanted me to have. But it was impossible at that time and I felt as if a great darkness enveloped me in that disappointment... Well, in hindsight, I probably gave place to the darkness with my disappointment! However, I sought God with great intensity and with much prayer and fasting until one day I was just so exhausted and so I lay down on the sofa to rest and even fell sleep! It was then all of a sudden that it seemed as if a GREAT LASER beam of Supernatural Light from Heaven burst into my hungry heart. It was so real that I dared not even breathe, let alone move!! Then the Spirit of God spoke deep into my spirit-man... "Gill, I am doing Laser-surgery on your heart." I literally felt the fingers of the Lord re-arranging my heart deep inside and even taking some stuff out!

I confess that sometimes it's difficult to put into words what happens at times like these, but it was as if the Holy Spirit was bringing something precious to birth in me even in that darkness. I even felt my breasts fill up as if there was milk overflowing as if to breastfeed a baby... such was the physical expression of God's laser beam surgery on my heart! From that time forward, ministry opportunities began to flood in and such a treasure was experienced from that dark time. You see, so often it is not the darkness that causes the pain but actually the **ABSENCE** of something that we need or long for or what God wants to give us. Yes! There are **"Treasures of Darkness"** for you RIGHT NOW!

But where does the Word of God fit in?

I have always believed that our experiences should be confirmed in the Word of God, so the Holy Spirit directed me into the very beginning!!! Genesis 1:1-3 says: "In the beginning GOD... WHO IS LIGHT... confronted, prepared, formed, fashioned and created the heavens and the earth. The earth was without form, an empty waste, and **GREAT DARKNESS was upon the face of the very great deep.** The Spirit of God was moving, hovering, brooding over the face of the waters. And God said: "Let there be LIGHT."

The Lord showed me that even though there was great darkness, this was not a hindrance or a problem to God! In fact, that darkness proved to be the ground for His wonderful creative ability as the Mighty Creator! So, He asked me, "Why was I always trying to avoid darkness?" It was obvious that I had to have a new revelation that treasure was going to come out of the dark times or situation! The Lord was waiting for me to discover the hidden riches of secret places and experience them in my own life... Hallelujah!

In the Word of God, the LIGHT came... that was the first Treasure to be revealed! Well, I thought it was! But then I was amazed that something had to happen BEFORE the Light came forth. Yes! The Spirit of God had to be involved! Oh, how this has helped me find the **"Treasures of Darkness"** in the dark times. It is crucial that FIRST The Spirit has to be allowed to hover, brood and be given the freedom for the WORD to come forth. Here we see the whole Triune God-Head in operation right there in the very beginning. Yes, God SAW the great darkness on the earth... but He had a plan! God always has a plan, that is why darkness is not a problem to God! I noticed that **The Spirit moved mightily upon the darkness and THEN the Word came**...The Father, The Spirit and The Living Word of God... the SON... they were ALL involved **AND EVERYTHING changed as LIGHT came!!**

"Treasures of Darkness" were brought forth in the very beginning! Hallelujah! So, for us as His Beloved children everything must change when we see darkness, difficulty, dryness or just impossible situations or a wilderness that seems unending like now... What should we do?

To find the Treasures of Darkness we must not panic!!

1) **See the Natural Facts**... don't try to hide from them... see that darkness as having NO power unless we give in to the distortions that the enemy brings in.
2) **Reject all Fears and Emotional Responses**...
3) **Recognise the Source and the enemy's plans**...
4) **Realize your need of the Holy Spirit to Move in power**... Invite the Holy Spirit to take full control as you yield to Him.
5) **Then SPEAK the Quickened Word of God**... It is written! Just like Jesus did when he was being tempted in the desert.
6) **THEN the Treasure will be revealed out of the darkness**... this is a principle that God showed me and even so much more!
7) **The LIGHT that came was not ordinary light... I believe that it was GLORY LIGHT as the Heavens Opened**... it was

not until the 4th day of Creation that the Lord created the Sun, Moon and Stars. That is our natural light, but the **"Treasures of Darkness"** that God promises us in His Word... produce **SUPERNATURAL LIGHT...**

Oh, don't miss this treasure that heaven will open over your dark, difficult situation... whatever it is; and He will bring His resources from Heaven to you. These are the **"Treasures of Darkness"**! It could be an amazing Grace, Revelation or Transformation in you or your family... it could be Healing or that special Peace that comes when the storm is raging about you, or even the Financial Provision that you desperately need. I don't know what **"Treasures of Darkness"** you need at this particular time, but I can promise you that they will come in a million different ways because of God's Promise, and He will keep His Word to you... He is The Faithful One! Have you wondered why? I am sure one of the most important reasons is that He simply loves us and knows we are safe when we are willing to always give God the Glory!

I am sure you are beginning, even now, to understand that we have no reason to be afraid of darkness and that there are beautiful Treasures and Hidden Riches there waiting for us to discover. As the old song says: "Turn your eyes upon Jesus, look full in His wonderful face and the things of earth will grow strangely dim IN THE LIGHT of His Glory and Grace! **Our perspective needs to change!**

BE LOOKING and EXPECTING for the hidden treasures!

Chapter 2.

Darkness is God's Opportunity

As we continue to search out the Treasures in Genesis Chapter 1... I realized that darkness seemed to be there BEFORE the light... **BUT GOD IS Light, and He was before ALL!** Well, I always knew that, but suddenly I saw it with new insight! The world, and sometimes us too, tends to look at it completely differently... we are devastated when we experience darkness or a challenging situation and our response is often that we feel as if the darkness or Satan has stolen our light, or our peace, or our provision, or our health, or a certain relationship with that precious person. **True???** We know the Word and remember that in John 10:10 Jesus said that, "The thief comes in order to steal and kill and destroy." So, if we are not careful, we can be joining in the BLAME Game for what we perceive as darkness being the enemy that has stolen from us, and it can certainly be that way??? Though not always! BUT then I remind myself that my Jesus has defeated the last enemy at the Cross and because of Jesus' victory it is possible for us to see it all quite differently!

The Holy Spirit doesn't see it negatively that way....**SO** if we are going to **"Receive the Treasures of Darkness"** that the Lord God has promised us in His Word, then you and I have to realize that we need to see things from God's perspective. We need to shift our vision! For instance, God often starts with the negative; just as He turns sorrow into Joy, He changes hopelessness into a Living Hope that will not disappoint; His Word is sent to bring healing from all sickness. The Word says: 1 Peter 2:24 "By His wounds you have been healed"

God starts with darkness it is His opportunity to demonstrate His power!

After all, He started His redeeming work with us when we were hidden in the utter darkness in the pit from which He drew us! Hallelujah! The Bible says in Isaiah 40:29 "He gives power to the weak, faint and weary and to him who has no might He increases strength. "Joel 3:1 "Let the weak say I am strong." He even brings Life out of death, doesn't He???

For God nothing is impossible!! Darkness is God's Opportunity!

Can you see that God, in His wisdom, often starts with darkness or a negative situation, some difficulty or a terrible hopeless circumstance or lack and THEN He releases the **"Treasures of Darkness?"** God's principle is that no matter what darkness comes into our lives **there are ALWAYS "Treasures of Darkness"** hidden to be discovered and to be experienced. In fact, in that particular Scripture it goes on to say there is even more in Isaiah 45: 3 **"AND hidden riches in secret places."**

My dear special friend if we believe God's Word and see from His viewpoint into the Heavenly Realm, **THEN EVERYTHING CAN CHANGE** because it is God's opportunity to demonstrate His power in our lives and bless us with more of Heavens Blessings poured out in His amazing generosity to us! Psalm 139: 11-12 says: "If I say: "Surely the darkness shall cover me and the night shall be the only light about me. Even the darkness hides nothing from you, but the night shines as day; **the darkness and the light are both alike to you."** WOW!! That is SO incredible!!

Another little discovery was that we find that in the beginning there was still darkness there, even when what appears to be the Glory Light was created by the spoken Word of God. God did not do away with darkness! In Genesis 1: 4 it says: "God separated the light from the darkness." We too, need to understand that we need to be separated from the darkness and THEN we can **"Receive the Treasures of Darkness"** and bring them into the light to Glorify God. 1Peter 2:9 "You are a chosen race, a royal priesthood, a dedicated nation, God's own purchased special people, that you may set forth the wonderful deeds and display the virtues and perfections of Him **who called you out of darkness into His marvellous light."** 2 Corinthians 4:6 "For God Who said "Let light shine out of the darkness" has shone in our hearts so as **to beam forth the Light** for the illumination of the knowledge of the majesty and glory of God in the face of Jesus Christ the Messiah."

Darkness has the ability to display God's beauty in our lives!

Have you ever looked in a Jeweller's Shop window? The Diamonds are always set out on a very black background and there are very bright lights focused from above! That enhances the sparkling beauty of the precious diamonds... YET these actual diamonds are found in the deep dark recesses of the earth below, sometimes 150- and 250-kilometres underground or even at times as much as 800 kilometres in the complete darkness of the volcanic rock! From there, they are brought to the surface as great chunks of ordinary rock. Then the process is a gentle crushing and then finally a SEPARATION between what is valuable and what is worthless.

We are God's beautiful Diamonds found in the deep dark pits of our sin and blackness of our lives lived without Him. The Bible says: Psalm 40: 2 "He drew me up out of a horrible pit, out of the miry clay and set my feet upon a rock." God says in John 3:16 "God SO greatly loved and dearly prized the world that He even gave up His only Begotten Son, so that whoever believes in Him shall not perish but have eternal life." God saw the darkness of the world and He loved it enough to send His Best Treasure into the darkness...YES! You are right, He sent His only Begotten Son Jesus Christ! He did this all for us so that we could become His Personal Treasures!

No wonder there are **"Treasures of Darkness" for us to discover!!**

For us to: **"Receive the Treasures of Darkness"** there will need to be a SEPARATION, just as God separated the Light from the darkness in the beginning... so we need to:

1) **See from God's Perspective**...AND we will need **NEW revelation** of who we are in Christ Jesus. Ephesians 2:6 "God raised us up together with Christ and made us sit down together with Him giving us joint-seating with Him in the Heavenly realm."
2) **Allow God to separate us from the darkness**... then we will not only receive the **"Treasures of Darkness"** but as I have said: actually BE His Treasures!!!

Darkness is God's Opportunity to reveal His Treasures so we can receive them!

Chapter 3.

The Spirit Reveals Hidden Treasures in ADAM!

So, we see, in the beginning God knew how to seize His opportunity when darkness filled the earth... But what about man? Where does he come in? Genesis 2:7 "Then the Lord God formed man from the dust of the ground and breathed into his nostrils the breath or spirit of life and man became a living being".

So for the first time I really saw that the original man... the first Adam, actually came out of the seeming darkness of the dust of the earth!

No wonder I needed a new and different understanding of darkness... it almost seemed as if it was God's delight to do what was absolutely impossible to man. A handful of dust from the darkness of the ground became the first Adam, son of God, and all because the Lord God actually breathed His breath into him! Could it be that for us to receive the **"Treasures of Darkness"** we too need the breath of God the Holy Spirit to breathe into us? I guess so!!

Some of you will have read my previous books where I have shared my testimony about when I died and went to Heaven? There in Heaven the fragrance was exquisite, the brightness of the colours vibrant and resplendent, the breeze soft and warm and everywhere there was this EXTRAORDINARY LIFE! The trees were SO alive and each leaf moving in harmony and expressing praise to its Creator. As I walked together with the Lord in the meadows of lush green grass, it was as if the Spirit whispered, "Look behind you Gill." I looked and I really expected to see the grass trampled down where we had walked. But to my amazement, as I watched, each single blade of grass popped back up and was overflowing with this extraordinary Supernatural Life... I couldn't see where we had walked, it was as if we were floating, suspended in another dimension of time and space. Yet at the same time, the Spirit said, "This is Eternal Life, nothing that is damaged, hurt, oppressed or wounded can ever stay down when they have My LIFE." Oh, the wonder and joy of being in His Presence... this was the most incredible HOME COMING! There was no way I ever wanted to leave...

BUT GOD! He had other plans as He spoke to me again... "Gill, I am sending you back to do the works I have prepared for you to do." My reaction was not at all gracious... "No Lord I want to stay here with you." I tell you, if only we knew how we endanger our very inner being when we say, "No to God." We immediately lose the sense of His Beautiful Presence, cutting ourselves off from that precious relationship and worse still, perhaps more than anything... we open the door for the enemy of our souls, Satan, to creep in and bring utter darkness and despair back into our lives! We give Satan permission to steal our joy and peace and everything else too.

Almost immediately I was plunged into what seemed like an everlasting tunnel of heavy almost tangible, oppressive blackness, like a dark hole that was sucking me down, down, down... I did not seem able to stop myself being drawn into this abyss. Somehow, I knew that it was the everlasting torment of Hell. Believe me! I have seen enough of that hell that has left an indelible mark on my life that I never want to see anyone ever go there... Hell was made for Satan and his demons. God never intended hell for us... we have been created to be His beloved children through believing in the perfect sacrifice of Christ on the Cross so that we can receive the free gift of Eternal Life and God can be with our Father in Heaven for ever and ever!!

Why I am telling you this? Because in the terror of this all-consuming darkness my spirit cried out again and for the only time in my life, I heard the audible voice of God! It was like no other voice... it was like running waters, clear, soft, tender, personal and overflowing with pure unending love... YET, at the same time, I have never experienced such authority and incredible power in a voice ever! So much so, that I know that whatever He would have said to me I would have done... even if it was to get up and walk off the operating table in the hospital... Yes! I would have done it and it would have happened; such was the commanding power with which He spoke. But He didn't say that, He just simply said, **"Gill I want you to Breath me IN as I count, One, Two Three."** I honestly breathed like never before, as if my very life depended upon it... and in that very same moment it was the Eternal Breath of God that I breathed in, and you could say, it was the Life-Giving Spirit of God Himself! It was THEN that the darkness completely disappeared and by the Grace of God it has never returned in that same horrific way.

It was only recently when I was preaching about the **"Treasures**

of Darkness" that the Lord reminded me of how He had breathed Life into me personally and IN that terrible darkness, that was the only time when I have heard His audible voice... **that Treasure of Darkness changed my life forever!!!** So, I am forever grateful that I experienced that excruciating terrible darkness, and that brought forth into my life the very best **"Treasures of Darkness!"** I really had never realized that particular treasure beforehand! Oh, the Lord is SO good that nothing is ever wasted in our lives!!

So, what about Adam?

Yes! God formed him from the seeming darkness of the dust of the ground and yet he went on to name all the livestock, wild and tame, all the birds of the air... He was overflowing and filled with SO much Life... Adam's name was the son of God! Luke 3:38... For fun, many years ago, Skippy and I tried to see how we got on in our imaginations naming some new creatures!!! It was IMPOSSIBLE but we had great fun and laughter erupted from within us as we tried to be creative like Adam... but to no avail!!! How we admired Adam as he worked with the Spirit of God!! **YET...** with all this Life within him, Adam still needed something else... he needed a companion, a helper, suitable, adapted and complementary for him.

So, what did God do?

The Bible tells us in Genesis 2:21-22 "The Lord God caused a deep darkness of sleep to fall upon Adam and while he slept He took one of his ribs or part of his flesh and closed it up. And the rib or part of the side which the Lord God had taken from the man He built up and made into a woman and He brought her to the man." We probably all know that Scripture really well, but the Holy Spirit has so wonderfully just pointed something special out to me, that in those particularly tough dark times God can be at work inside us!! He knows what treasure is potentially hidden deep inside us that is ready to be brought forth into the light at just the right time!! This has greatly encouraged me to be able to respond positively and then to:

"Dare to Receive Treasures of Darkness."

When the Lord God caused that great deep darkness of sleep to come upon Adam... Adam had no idea what was in him... it took God to be at work in the darkness to pull out of him... the woman! Then Adam had to accept and receive the woman so that they could become one flesh!

I believe that inside each one of us... there are hidden treasures of unlimited potential waiting to be discovered!

Maybe it could be more of the likeness of the Character of Christ in you or me, or Ministries, Spiritual Gifts, Fruits of the Spirit, or even a partner for life! Or even to write a book?!!! Unlimited potential needs to be developed and SO MUCH MORE that God has planned for us to do and be... so that we will be able to produce lasting fruit for our Father and He will be Glorified... it's all hidden inside us for us to discover!!

God knows what He wants to bring out of us at every stage of our journey with Him and He is always ready to give us **"Treasures of Darkness"** as we respond to Him. The Lord does not want us to try to run away from the darkness or complain or be fearful, and definitely not to see it as something negative to be avoided! But we are to be looking with great expectation for those **"Treasures of Darkness"**. We see this very clearly when Jesus was tempted in the wilderness by Satan; God was at work in that dark wilderness time, even for Jesus when the going got really tough for Him... we are told angels came and strengthened Jesus and He demonstrated to us how to overcome the enemy by: "It is written."

Were there "Treasures of Darkness" there for Jesus in the wilderness?

YES! Luke 4:14 "He came out in the power of the Spirit and the fame of Him spread through the whole region round about". The beautiful thing is that those very **"Treasures of Darkness"** are now ours in Christ Jesus as we receive them into our lives! Jesus has modelled the life in the Holy Spirit, and He wants us to **"Receive Amazing Treasures of Darkness"** so we can give them to others to bring Glory to God, and our creative potential is brought forth and released out of our innermost being. You and I, like Adam, have no idea what God has planted in us... maybe just now it's just a very small seed, but the darkness is God's opportunity to bring it out into the open if we **"Dare to Receive the Treasures of Darkness"**.

I asked the Lord for an illustration from my own life and immediately I remembered how one of the women of God keep saying to me, "Have you written that book yet Gill?" Every time she said it, I cringed and thought: "No way would I ever be able to do that!!!" But there came a time when there was a really challenging situation in my life and I didn't know how to get through, yes you could call it darkness... Until one day I was watching a children's video: "Rescuers down Under" with our young grandsons as they were then! When suddenly I saw an eagle in captivity on an enormous rock and the Holy Spirit spoke to me... "Go and tell my people they are Eagles and not Chickens grovelling on the ground." Write a book about how they can "Dare to be an Eagle." And so, God began pulling out of me what I had no idea was deep inside my spirit-man!!! And, friends, He is still doing just that, right now in this Lockdown situation we are all experiencing!

Hallelujah, God loves to bring out the "Treasures of Darkness."

Chapter 4.

Treasures of Rescue and Breakthrough for NOAH!

As we move on in the Word of God, the Holy Spirit led me to... **NOAH.** Genesis Chapter 6:5-6 "The Lord saw that the wickedness of man was great in the earth and the Lord regretted that He had made man on the earth, and He was grieved at heart." But God says in Genesis Chapter 6:8 "But Noah found grace and favour in the eyes of the Lord."

This terrible, wicked situation must have deeply touched and saddened the heart of the Lord God and yet God found one man in the darkness... Hallelujah! Yes, He found NOAH to be righteous and because of that God had a plan to rescue His creation. The Word tells us that the Lord God spoke to Noah in Genesis 7:1 and the Lord God said to Noah, "Come with all your household into the ARK, for I have seen you to be righteous in this generation". In verse 4 The Lord goes on to say, "For in seven days I will cause it to rain upon the earth forty days and forty nights and every living substance and thing that I have made I will destroy, blot out, and wipe away from the face of the earth".

Suddenly I saw the **"Treasures of Darkness"** yes it was the ARK!!! But for Noah and his household to find this treasure... he needed to be obedient! The Word says in verse 5 "And Noah did all that the Lord commanded him". I personally do not think it was at all easy for Noah... some people would not have understood what he was doing. A boat like the Ark had never been needed before or ever built before... and it took approximately 60-70 years... some people estimate it was as much as 120 years! Whatever; it was not easy and probably the most difficult thing Noah had ever tackled in his 600 years!! That is how old Noah was when the flood waters came upon the earth!

Sometimes the Lord asks us to do things that other people will not understand and that always means really trusting that you have heard from God in the face of opposition and not being swayed or becoming double minded. Has this happened to you too? James 1:6 "Not wavering or hesitating and become as a wave tossed by the wind." Noah was certainly single-minded and made the Ark in all the exact dimensions and details according to the Lord's instructions. That ensured that he and his family were able to experience the **"Treasures of Darkness"** and even all the animals too! They were wonderfully rescued from total annihilation.

As I pondered these things, The Holy Spirit has given me even more revelation that is hidden in the Word of God! Genesis 7:11 "In the year 600 of Noah's life, in the seventeenth day of the second month, that same day all **THE FOUNTAINS of the great deep darkness were broken up and burst forth, and the windows and floodgates of the heavens were opened."** I have read that many times but missed the **"Treasures of Darkness"**!!

Just BEFORE the rains came for forty days and nights something else happened... we read that **from the GREAT DEEP DARKNESS... there came a surprising breakthrough from underneath.** There was a bursting forth, a surge of unknown, unexpected fountains that LIFTED the ARK up and floated it!!!! Nobody knew those waters were there hidden in that great deep darkness, but it was those waters bursting forth from those fountains that enabled the ARK to fulfil its purpose to save Noah and his family! If the rains had come first it would have been submerged, land-locked and never fulfilled God's plan.

Breakthrough came from the great darkness and even more... the windows and floodgates of the heavens were opened!

YES! **"Treasures of Darkness"** were released from the unknown hidden fountains of the great deep but **ALSO** from above came the blessings of the Heavenly Realm that kept them safe for those forty days and forty nights. You could say there were: **"Double Treasures of Darkness"**! Noah was really blessed and because of his obedience, all his family too **"Received the Treasures of Darkness"**! God does this with us: in the darkest of hours there are always **"Treasures of Darkness"** bursting forth from hidden places, miraculous provision and unexpected sources that will lift us up and bring God's special blessing into our lives, even if we have messed up! God promises **we will be RESCUED and experience the BREAKTHROUGH we need to get through**... just like Noah and his family!

I would like to share a couple of illustrations from our own lives where that has happened to us. Several years ago, we were invited to serve on the Good News Crusade Team in Malvern. It was a tremendous privilege and we took it very seriously in our preparation for the Camp week. At the time we were Pastors in our own first Church in Buxton in Derbyshire. It was a steep learning curve as we left our Bible College Training at Roffey Place, (which is now Kingdom Faith,) with Colin Urquhart and the late Bob Gordon. Buxton was our first real experience of laying down our lives for our congregation, so we were eagerly growing in our faith walk and happy not to be paid a salary. We were learning to trust God for everything, and it was a glorious adventure!!

So, we came to the GNC Camp full of expectation and during the week there was a particular appeal for finances that really touched our hearts. Skippy and I agreed as we prayed that we should give everything we had in our possession. We were sowing our only £20 in faith as that was all we had at the time! The week ended and on the Saturday morning we suddenly realized that the car's petrol tank was on empty and we had no money at all! It was in the days when we didn't have a bank card. OH! Panic swept over us… had we not heard God right about giving everything into the offering? Had we been irresponsible and foolish? It felt like a really desperately dark situation! We even thought, maybe God would fill up the car with petrol supernaturally as He had done once before? Our minds were going in overtime as you can guess… but no answers came; and by this time we had completely lost our peace, as you can imagine!!

So, after praying, asking forgiveness of the Lord we decided to set off across the field towards the exit gate. I can't say we were in faith… just desperate for the Lord to get us out of this dark situation… All at once, as we approached the gate, we saw a tall figure waving at us… we waved back, saying "Bye" and realized it was Don Double himself. As he continued to wave, we noticed he had a piece of what we thought was a piece of paper in his hand. We stopped and Don came over and said, "God told me to urgently give you this before you left the Campsite." He handed us an envelope. As we received the envelope, Don said, "I have never done this before, but the Holy Spirit impressed on me very strongly that I was to bless you; I started to write a cheque, but the Spirit said No… it had to be cash… so here you are, do receive the Lord's blessing for whatever is your need".

As you can imagine, Skippy and I gratefully received the envelope from Don and to our amazement we were utterly overwhelmed as we opened the envelope to see that the Holy Spirit had truly blessed us. Inside was £100 in cash! Both Skippy and I wept in thanksgiving as we knew we certainly did not deserve such an over-whelming blessing! So, as you can guess we were able to put petrol in the car and we went home rejoicing and singing praises, knowing that we had just received…

An amazing Rescue and a Breakthrough as God gave us unexpected...
"Treasures of Darkness."

God's promises are certainly never fulfilled because of our actions or our working hard to see them come to pass... No! It is sheer Grace and Mercy and the Lord Himself honouring His Word in His faithfulness and Goodness... simply because we are His children! What a Loving Heavenly Father He is!!

The other testimony of Rescue and Breakthrough....

This occurred when we moved here to Mallorca. We had agreed with the Vendor that we would pay the whole amount for our apartment by the 1st of August... if not we would pay 20% over and above. This seemed very reasonable back in the February! But our house didn't sell... we had arranged to ship all our furniture out and were due to leave UK on July 12th. Oh! Oh! Oh! Such a stretchy time, but to our delight a young woman from the Church came and agreed to buy the house; that was in May! Hallelujah, she was a first-time buyer and there should be no problems with a mortgage. She moved in as we left UK, all of us confident that everything would be alright!

However, sometimes God's timing and ours do not coincide! Sandra, who was purchasing our house, had some stupid unforeseen difficulties with her Mortgage Company... so everything was delayed for months! In the meantime, we had arrived in our new apartment here in Palma and soon it was July 31st... I can tell you the darkness just seemed to envelope us!!! Skippy and I again repented of the foolishness of agreeing to pay the extra 20% after August 1st because we certainly had no extra finance after all the expenses of moving out here. So that night we wept, we pleaded with the Lord for His mercy but, in the natural, we could see no way how He could deliver us out of this predicament.

Once again... **BUT GOD... He had "Treasures of Darkness"** hidden away for us! At 8.30am the next morning August 1st an Inspector came to the door. This is normal here in Spain, every new building has to be inspected to receive the certificate that all is ok. Our hearts were trembling in fear when he came back to our front door! He told us that apparently the top flat had put in a fireplace that was not on the original plan... so he couldn't pass the building! That meant we did not need to pay until that fireplace was removed and the building re-inspected!! How we rejoiced that once again the Lord had rescued us and opened up a way from a really dark situation! The answer was literally from nowhere that we could ever have worked out... God opened the fountains from the very great deep darkness and gave us **"Treasures of Darkness".** What the Lord has done for us, He will do for you... it's His Promise!

"Treasures of Darkness" will be there for you too as you step out in Faith!

Chapter 5.

Treasures of Darkness are Received by Faith for ABRAHAM!

As I continued to go treasure hunting with the Holy Spirit, He stopped me next with **Abram**. In Genesis 15:1 it says: **"After these things"** What things? Were they important?

Let's find out about ABRAHAM!

Well Abram, as he was before The Lord changed his name, has just had a tremendous victory over the combined kings of Chedorlaomer when he had rescued Lot, his cousin, his women and all his possessions that the kings had captured. Abram had even had a very special meeting with Melchizedek, King of Salem, representing Christ, who had blessed Abram because the Most High God had given Abram victory over his foes. So, as a result, Abram had given him a tenth of all he had taken as the spoils from the victory, but he refused to take anything from the king of Sodom.

Sometimes after a great experience with the Lord or a tremendous Encounter with The Holy Spirit, there can be a period of darkness. Please don't think it has to be that way, but don't be surprised if it does happen... God often has a certain work to do in our lives, and remember:

God works his best works in darkness!

SO, we always need to remember that the Holy Spirit's mission in us is to transform us into the likeness of Christ! Paul says in Philippians 1:6 "I am convinced and sure of this very thing, that He Who began a good work in you will continue until the day of Jesus Christ, right up to the time of His return, developing and perfecting and bringing to full completion in you." So, I wonder what The Lord wanted to do in Abram after his great victory?

God always has a specific agenda and is going to continue the work He has started in Abram even after his super victories and an incredible meeting with Melchizedek! It's just like us... The Holy Spirit carries on working deep inside us!!! **SO, NOW... after these things...** There is a personal chat between The Lord and Abram! I encourage you to take time for these personal chats with the Holy Spirit!

Genesis 15:1-6 The Lord came to Abram in a vision, saying, "Fear not, Abram, I am your shield, your abundant compensation, and your reward shall be exceedingly great." And Abram said, "Lord God, what can you give me, since I am going from this world childless and he who shall be the owner and heir of my house is this steward Eliezer of Damascus?" And Abram continued, "Look, You have given me no child; and a servant born in my own house is my heir".

And behold, the word of the Lord came to him, saying: "This man shall not be your heir, but he who shall come from your own body shall be your heir". And the Lord brought Abram outside his tent into the starlight and said: "Look now toward the heavens and count the stars... if you are able to number them?" Then He said to him... "So shall your descendants be".

"Abram believed, trusted in, relied on, and remained steadfast to the Lord
and it was counted to him as righteousness."

The Holy Spirit had exposed in Abram that there was a deep under-lying darkness and hidden fear oppressing him... **he had no heir!** So, when the Lord appears and tells Abram, "Do not fear" The Lord is addressing this deep-seated problem, and confronts Abram and brings it out into the light where God can do His miraculous works. God always wants us to stop looking at the problems and to get our eyes lifted from where we are and to look at God Himself. He knows that is the only way that we will be able to receive the **"Treasures of Darkness"**! in our personal, particular, challenging circumstances.

So, the Lord says to Abram: "I AM your shield, and abundant compensation and your great reward". Then, like many of us, Abram does not seem to appreciate what the Lord has just said to him and how very gracious God is being. I guess the reason is because he is consumed by the obstacle and can only see the difficulty, and the darkness has distorted things, and he only sees the impossibility of having no personal heir.

Oh, Lord, how exceedingly good you are to us!

We too are so often consumed by the darkness that we begin to tell the Lord what He already knows, and here we see that Abram proceeds to do exactly that... just like us! We so easily forget that God knows everything before we even say a word!!!... How foolish we can be, but how amazing is His patience with us! It is good for us to see how the Lord gently draws Abram into that place where things could change, and he could begin to **"Receive the Treasures of Darkness"** awaiting him.

Twice Abram complains to the Lord and I suppose he is really in a way blaming The Lord because He has not given him a proper heir. Abram says, "I am going from this world childless." And he continues speaking to the Lord saying, "Look, You have given me no child and a servant born in my house is my heir". Abram only sees Eliezer, his servant, as an heir and this is the big problem... This is the situation and it is not what he wants! In other words, Abram is completely deaf and blind spiritually to the wonderful promise that the Lord is speaking personally to him when He says, "This man shall not be your heir, but he who shall come from your own body".

Let us find out where the "Treasures of Darkness" are

God literally brings Abram outside into the darkness of the night sky and tells him to... "Look now toward the heavens and count the stars if you are able to number them?" Then the Lord speaks as Abram is trying to count the stars... "So shall your descendants be from your own body." And we are told **Abram believed God and it was counted to him as righteousness.** Oh WOW! A miracle happened as Abram looked up!! Doesn't it speak volumes to us? We need to learn from Abram! Looking up to the Supernatural God in the Heavens is a MUST! That completely changes Abram's perspective and it will change ours too, I promise you!

At a certain time in our lives, Skippy and I were facing another impossible situation and there seemed no way out yet again!! We had been given a prophetic word from a man we highly respected, who had no idea of the challenges we were facing. So, we took the word very seriously! This is what it was:

"Go out into the darkness of the night and under the stars completely surrender your whole lives to the Lord... individually, your marriage, your family and the ministry." It proved to be harder to do than it would appear! Because here in a city like Palma, there is too much artificial light so the stars cannot be seen easily, and it needs to be a really clear night! But eventually it all came together and with many tears of absolute surrender we both handed everything back to the Lord. It was one of those times when we knew that things were going to rapidly change and yes, they did!! In that simple act of obedience and faith God was able to bring **"Treasures of Darkness"** into our lives. In fact, I would say that we would not be living here in Mallorca, nor have the ministry that has developed over the last 20 years if we had not obeyed the word that was given to us! Something significant happened in the spiritual realm as we believed God's word to us and a little like Abram... our obedience was credited to us as righteousness! All Glory to the Father of the Lord Jesus Who saw our hearts and we stepped into the **"Treasures of Darkness"** that the Holy Spirit had prepared for us...Hallelujah!

But that wasn't the end of the story with Abram... God often tests our faith... not to destroy it, but to prove it! Peter himself says in 1 Peter 1: 6-7 "Though now for a little while you may be distressed by trials and suffer temptations, so that the genuineness of your faith may be tested, which is infinitely more precious than perishable gold which is tested by fire. This proving of your faith is intended to redound to your praise and glory and honour when Jesus the Christ is revealed."

Abram did not speak Isaac into existence, God did!

Abram simply believed what God said and then he acted upon the promise, as a result Isaac was born. Romans 4:19-20 "Not being weak in faith, he did not consider his own body, already dead because he was about 100 years old, or the deadness of Sarah's womb. He did not waver at the promise of God through unbelief, but was strengthened in faith, giving glory to God, and being fully convinced that what He had promised He was able to perform."

Like Abram, our faith must be in God, not in our faith or in anybody else! In and of itself, faith has no creative power, faith affirms what already exists in the unseen world and in what God has said and promised, knowing that in His time it will come to pass because it is His will. So, whatever you claim by faith must be based on what God has clearly promised to you in His Word. For you to **"Receive the Treasures of Darkness"** you need to see it in the Word of God!!

So what did The Lord do?

Abram had believed the promise from The Lord... but now God was going to cement the promise in actually making Covenant. Genesis 15:12 tells us: "When the sun was setting, a deep sleep overcame Abram, and **a horror of great darkness assailed and oppressed him"**.

God had to make sure that Abram really did believe that he would have the descendants that would multiply in all the earth. Abram was even forewarned prophetically that his descendants would be slaves, strangers and temporary residents in the land of Egypt for 400 years, but in the 4th generation they would come back to the land of Canaan."

THEN… The Lord literally **CUT COVENANT** as the sun was going down and a thick darkness came up and a smoking oven appeared, and a flaming torch passed between the pieces of the sacrificial animals. We are told that on the same day that the Lord made a covenant, He spoke the promise to Abram, saying, "To your descendants I have given this land forever." Yes! **"Treasures of Darkness"** were revealed to Abram, not just for him but for all his generations to come. That is what happens when we believe what God says!! **Did it end there? No!** Abram, like us, messed things up again and again. At one time Abram foolishly listened to Sarai, his wife, who thought she had a good idea!

Beware of good ideas that don't come from God!

The result was that a son, Ishmael was born to Hagar, his Egyptian maidservant. Abram was deceived that this would be the child that the Lord had promised him several years earlier. Disaster! **But still, faithfully, God had "Treasures of Darkness" hidden away for Abram! What an AMAZING God!!!**

So, we pick up the story in Genesis 17:1-8 "The Lord appeared to Abram again when he was 99 years old. This time it was to re-establish the Covenant that He had already made with Abram… but this time The Lord would also give greater details and change his name from Abram to ABRAHAM… from "exalted father" to "father of a multitude". This time there was an added promise as well that Abraham would be exceedingly fruitful and even kings would come from his posterity. It was promised specifically that Sarai, herself, would have a son with Abraham. So now the Lord God having re-named Abram to Abraham, He now changed "Sarai" to become "Sarah" meaning Princess! If you can see it:

"Treasures of Darkness" are again beginning to flow!

The Lord was transforming both Abraham and Sarah to be the vessels that would fulfil His plans and purposes! How wonderful is that? So, in Genesis 21:1-3 "The Lord visited Sarah, as He had said, and the Lord did for her as He had promised. For Sarah became pregnant and bore

Abraham a son in his old age, at the set time God had told him. Abraham named his son, whom Sarah bore to him, Isaac meaning laughter." Mind you, earlier the Lord had had to send three angels to convince Sarah that this would happen and they both laughed at the impossibility! No wonder Isaac's name means laughter!! Sarah was 90 years old and well past child-bearing age and Abraham 99 years old with a withered body we are told!

BUT GOD......The Lord said in Genesis 18:14
"Is anything too hard or too wonderful for the Lord?

You see, as we have followed Abraham's journey of faith, we have seen SO many illustrations of **"Treasures of Darkness"** overtake his life. In spite of all his failures, nothing could stop the Lord God fulfilling His Word that out of the dark situations **there are always "Treasures of Darkness"** waiting for us to discover and by the help of the Holy Spirit appropriate them into our lives so that we can walk by faith and not by sight.

Throughout Abraham's life there were many other situations of
pain and he
experienced great darkness.

One example is when God told Abraham to listen to Sarah his wife when she said, "Cast out this bondwoman and her son, for the son of this bondwoman shall not be an heir with my son Isaac." Abraham had to send Hagar and Ishmael away because only in Isaac would his posterity be. **How hard was that?** Yet all the time Abraham had God's Covenant promise and he continued to trust and walk by faith even when it seemed impossible.

No wonder Abraham is called our father of faith!

Then, I suppose the greatest darkness of all must have been when God tested and proved Abraham. We are told in Genesis 22:1-18 "God said, take now your son, your only son Isaac, whom you love, and go to the region of Moriah and offer him there as a burnt offering upon one of the mountains of which I will tell you." In this supreme test, God was proving whether Abraham really did fear and revere God... and YES! There was Divine intervention as Abraham took the knife to kill his own son Isaac. At that moment the Angel of the Lord called to him, "Abraham, Abraham! Do not lay your hand on the lad or do anything to him, for now I know that you fear and revere God, since you have not held back from me your son, your only son". We are told Abraham looked up and saw a ram held captive in the thicket by its horns and then he offered that ram as the sacrifice instead of his son.

Such was God's pleasure in Abraham that the Angel of the Lord declared in Genesis 22:17-18...

"In blessing, I will bless you and in multiplying, I will multiply your descendants like the stars of the heavens and as the sand on the seashore and your SEED (Heir) will possess the gate of His enemies. And in your Seed (Christ) shall all the nations of the earth be blessed and by Him bless themselves because you have heard and obeyed my voice."

I find this amazing, that Mount Moriah was the place of sacrifice where Abraham dedicated his only son Isaac to the Lord **AND YES**... it is the exact same place where Jesus the Only Begotten Son of God became our perfect sacrifice all those years later when Mount Moriah became Calvary! Isn't that SO wonderful?!

This was the very first time that God's own Holy Covenant Name **"Jehovah Jireh"** was manifested! Abraham was chosen to have this very amazing revelation: No wonder this is a prophetic sign as well as a special revelation of the Person of God Himself.

"The LORD IS PROVIDER!"

God reveals Himself to Abraham and **"Treasures of Darkness"** flood into his life AND these treasures flow to us too as we put our faith in Christ and we are given a full assurance that in Christ Jesus we have everything for life and godliness. 2 Peter 2:3...YES! In Christ, the Messiah, we too, **"Receive the Treasures of Darkness"** won for us, as we put our faith in Christ the Spotless Lamb of God sacrificed for us at Calvary. That is the best news you will ever hear and the greatest **"Treasure of Darkness"**.

If the Lord God could do that for Abraham, then He will be faithful to you too!

Chapter 6.

Treasures in the Places of Training

and Promotion for JOSEPH!

The Bible is full of exciting illustrations of how God takes an individual through some terrible, dark circumstances in order to prepare that person to be able to receive the most amazing **"Treasures of Darkness"** out of the secret hiding places of His purposes!

JOSEPH is one of those!

In Genesis 37:3-11 we read that Joseph was especially loved and favoured by his father Israel; so much so, that Israel had made a very special distinctive colourful coat for his beloved son. This, and the dreams Joseph had, caused a real hatred among all his brothers and you could say it was a very bitter sibling rivalry! Was Joseph wise when he repeated the dreams to his brothers? Probably not… on the second occasion even his father rebuked him, and then we are told that Joseph's brothers hated him even more with such envy and great jealousy that they wanted to kill him.

That is never an easy situation in the family to say the least! The enemy, Satan, made sure that things escalated as the brothers planned to find a way to kill Joseph. The on-going circumstances led to them actually capturing Joseph and throwing him into the pit out in the desert at Dothan. A hopeless dark place… could there be **"Treasures of Darkness"** for Joseph to get out of the pit and have his life saved?

YES! Rescue came in an unexpected way from a travelling caravan of Midianites from Gilead who just happened to come by on their camels on their way to Egypt to sell their produce. So, the brothers decided to sell Joseph to them for twenty pieces of silver. Then the brothers took Joseph's special coat, dipped it in a wild animal's blood and deceived their father Israel that Joseph had been killed by a wild animal. What terrible jealousy and envy that caused so much heartache!

I was trying to recall any time in our lives that something similar had happened to us… but you will be glad to know nothing as awful has happened in our lives! But I do personally know of family siblings that have a divided and heart-broken family situation through jealousy and misunderstandings that have led to total breakdown of any communication for years… it is so sad! How the enemy loves to destroy families and bring division, we need to make sure we carefully guard our family relationships as precious from The Lord. So, we must make sure that forgiveness and prayers continue to flow so the Holy Spirit can work His miracles and also keep reaching out with the love of God, remembering that His love will never fail.

I suppose the nearest I have ever experienced was at the beginning when I was radically saved and neither my mother nor my father could understand what had happened. I guess, like Joseph, I was not at all wise in my sharing and this led to great difficulty in our relationships… but nothing as dramatic as Joseph thankfully!! However, I am thrilled to be able to say that the Holy Spirit brought complete reconciliation in a most beautiful and supernatural way. Both of them became Born Again in the last moments of their lives. That is the mercy of the loving Father Himself; I am forever deeply grateful! If you have a difficulty in your family relationships, ask the Holy Spirit to lead you and He will surely show you where the **"Treasures of Darkness"** can be discovered and experienced personally as they are there waiting to be revealed to you!

Meanwhile, in Genesis 39:1-23 we read that Joseph was sold as a slave in Egypt to Pharaoh's chief officer called Potiphar. To begin with, all went really well for Joseph; his boss, Potiphar, recognized that Joseph was favoured because The Lord was with him… so he promoted Joseph to be supervisor in charge of his whole household. **"Treasures of Darkness"** were again beginning to flow to Joseph as he found great favour, and blessings were being experienced in spite of his slave status.

However, the enemy was scheming and used Potiphar's wife to continually try and get Joseph to lie with her. Although he refused day after day to give in to her temptations, she eventually took advantage when no one was around and grabbed his coat and screamed that Joseph had tried to rape her.

The result was that Joseph suddenly found himself in prison.

Sometimes in life, things do happen that are totally unfair and yet that is when we need to believe that God is still in full control; make sure you keep our spirit right and believe that The Holy Spirit is working behind the scenes, looking after us and preparing and training us for our future destiny. Yet we read once again there are unexpected **"Treasures of**

Darkness" for Joseph even right there in the darkness of the prison. It is written in the Word of God that the warden of the prison recognized that The Lord was with Joseph and, because of this, gave him special favour actually there in the prison; and once again Joseph was raised up and he was put in charge of all the other prisoners. Then we read that God made whatever he did to prosper.

WOW! That is really amazing "Treasures of Darkness!"

I wonder if you can see how the Holy Spirit has been **TRAINING** Joseph in every dark situation and all through his difficult life experiences. All the time, The Lord is with him and gives Joseph that special favour and every time he is **PROMOTED.**

Joseph was lifted out of death in the pit, he was made a slave but raised up to be in charge of the whole household of Potiphar and now even though he has been unjustly put in prison for something he did not do... **YET**, even there the Lord the Holy Spirit equips Joseph so that a visible favour rests upon him and the warden promotes him.

Joseph is being trained in leadership in every situation!

At times we may not be able to see the bigger picture, but God, in these times of darkness is training us and He knows how to promote us even though we might get impatient... as even Joseph did! There, in that very dark prison time, Joseph's special God-given gift of interpreting dreams was developed using the two prisoners who had dreams on the same night... the Baker and the Butler. You can read the details in Genesis 40:1-23 how Joseph interpreted their dreams correctly as both the Baker and the Butler had dreams. The outcome was that the Butler was restored to serve as the King's Cupbearer to the Pharaoh while the Baker was beheaded.

But God's timing took two more years for Joseph to be released!

Joseph must have thought he was forgotten deep in the darkness of the prison dungeons, yet the time came when God gave the Pharaoh dreams that no one could interpret... it was then that the Butler suddenly remembered Joseph! THEN... in just one day, all the years of preparation and training came to fulfilment and the real promotion happened. Genesis 41:12-43 gives us the full story of how Joseph interpreted Pharaoh's dreams and how he was elevated and made head over all the land of Egypt and ultimately saved all of Egypt and his own family from disaster during the time of famine.

God had prepared Joseph for such a time as this!

As I was pondering Joseph's journey, I could see clearly how the Lord was training and preparing Joseph for his destiny, when eventually he would become ruler in Egypt. However, I knew I was missing something important... Suddenly, I realized that I had overlooked the importance of those dreams God had given Joseph right in the beginning!

It was because of those very dreams that Joseph had had all those years ago that he must have had a deep assurance that "Treasures of Darkness" would actually come to him at some time... because God is faithful to His word!

Joseph had the dreams about his bothers bowing down to him, and those dreams had to be fulfilled even when things looked impossible! We need to be assured that we too can stand on God's word and it will come to pass! Hallelujah, how wonderful is that?

Oh, my beloved one, as you are reading this, let faith arise and know that what God did for Joseph He can do for you too. In whatever situation.... whether it was a foolish decision that landed you in trouble, a heart-breaking family situation, or a totally unfair circumstance... God has a way out for you!!! I promise you that God's Word will not fail... He says,

"I will give you "Treasures of Darkness" and hidden riches in secret places that
you may know that it is I, The Lord, the God of Israel...
Who calls you by your name."

Finally, many years later, Joseph experienced every single detail that was revealed in his dreams that he had had as a boy; they all came true as the brothers all bowed down before him, desperate for food. Besides that, there was ultimately that special reconciliation with his blood brother Benjamin and eventually his father too.

Joseph had been trained and promoted in every part of his journey!

Joseph grew from the young exuberant boyhood potential to

fulfilment in manhood at thirty years old when he became ruler over the whole land of Egypt. What seemed impossible was brought about by the power of God moving in every circumstance as the darkness and difficulties actually trained and promoted Joseph to be ready for his destiny!

How did Joseph view it?

His brothers were afraid after Israel, their father, died that Joseph had not really forgiven them, and they offered to be his slaves. They must still have been feeling the guilt of what they had done all those years ago because they had obviously not forgiven themselves! But Joseph said in Genesis 50:19-21, "Fear not; for am I in the place of God? Vengeance is His, not mine. As for you, you meant it for evil against me, but God meant it for good, to bring about that many people should be kept alive, as they are this day. Now therefore, do not be afraid. I will provide for you and support you and your little ones. And he comforted them imparting cheer, hope, strength and spoke kindly to their hearts."

My plea to you today, and myself, is that we will respond willingly to the Lord Himself and take courage. We always need to make sure that our spirit is right with God and with others as well as ourselves. As you are reading these words, be sure that you have forgiven yourself for anything that is in your past... so that the enemy cannot condemn you! Then you will be able to believe that you will always have that deep assurance that He will bring you through to personally experience those:

"Treasures of Darkness" waiting for you and me around the corner!

Chapter 7.

Supernatural Treasures of Deliverance and Miracles for MOSES!

As the Holy Spirit took me for this walk through the Bible, I became fascinated that everywhere... well, that is what it seemed to me! God appeared to do His best work in dark situations! It was obvious that darkness was never a problem to God!!

So, we are going to explore the secrets surrounding MOSES!

Exodus 1 tells us that Joseph had died and that there was now a new king who was intimidated and threatened by the way that the Israelites were so rapidly increasing... so he ordered that God's people would be given great burdens and severe slavery and afflicted by Taskmasters set over them. But we read that the more the Egyptians oppressed them, the more they increased; because God's favour was upon them!! That was when the king ordered that every son born to the Hebrew women must be killed and cast into the River Nile.

Great darkness, great heartache... What would God do?

Here in Exodus 1:15-21 God does something completely unexpected to reveal the **"Treasures of Darkness"**! Two midwives, Puah which means: Joy to parents; and Shiprah which means shining light... were ordered to kill every male baby boy born to the Hebrew women... BUT they feared God and did not do as the king had commanded. Sometimes treasures come in the circumstances and at other times... it's a person or people! What treasures these two midwives were, so courageous; and God blessed them with families of their own because they honoured God. This reminded me that our beautiful Holy Spirit has a similar role in our lives as our Midwife!

Let me explain... The Holy Spirit was there in the very beginning of Creation bringing forth the Word and then Light came. The Holy Spirit was also there in our very beginning... He brought forth the revelation of the Saviour Jesus Christ! The Spirit of God convicted us of our great need of Salvation! Yes! The Spirit was the Midwife who attended us as we were Born Again... birthing us spiritually from darkness to light, from hopelessness to a hope that will never disappoint!

One of the roles of the Holy Spirit is to ensure there is real bonding with our Heavenly Father as a child of God... in the same way a midwife helps the baby find the mother's breast to suck the milk! So, The Holy Spirit draws us to the breast of El Shaddai so that we can learn to draw nourishment from the full-breasted One Himself. He is the Life-Giving Spirit who makes sure we are breathing deeply as we begin our new life as a new creation in The Lord Jesus Christ. In the natural, the midwife cuts the umbilical cord to separate the baby from the mother... so in the Spiritual realm The Holy Spirit separates us from the dominion of darkness and transfers us into the Kingdom of God's Son.

This partnership with the Holy Spirit is glimpsed here in this passage and it may help us to appreciate the incredible work God has done in our lives to reveal **"The Treasures of Darkness"** that we may never have really understood. How precious that God had these two God-fearing midwives there to save so many Hebrew baby boys!

So, where does Moses fit in?

We are told in Exodus 2:1-10 that Moses, when he was born, was an exceedingly beautiful baby, born to a godly couple called Amram and Jochebed who were of the priestly tribe of Levi. I wondered how his mother Jochebed would have felt when she looked at her precious son for the very first time? Knowing that according to the king's law he had to be cast into the River Nile to die... **BUT** according to God he was destined to bring deliverance to God's people.

I believe that in that crisis of great darkness, the Holy Spirit must have opened Jochebed's eyes to see Moses with supernatural vision as to just how special he was... so she did everything she could to hide him for three months! However, there came a time when it was no longer possible to keep him hidden; so she made an ark for him out of bulrushes and papyrus, making it water proof by daubing the ark with bitumen and pitch... and then put Moses in it and laid it among the bulrushes at the brink of the Nile.

Some of us who are mothers can only possibly guess at the depth of anguish Jochebed must have gone through to actually make that decision to let Moses go! **YET** if she hadn't, then his deliverance would not have come from the most unexpected source of Pharaoh's daughter, who drew Moses out of the water and brought him up as her own son! The treasure for Jochebed was amazing... God had already planned that she was going to be asked and blessed to breastfeed Moses and look after him for Pharaoh's daughter, and that she would even be rewarded with wages to do this! Only God could have orchestrated such a deliverance from certain death!

Oh, what wonderful "Treasures of Darkness" came from nowhere!
       Much later on, we read how Moses tried, in his own strength to become the deliverer of God's people. In our everyday language... Moses blew it! So, in fear for his life he took refuge in the land of Midian where he married Zipporah and had two sons and looked after his father-in-law's flock of sheep in the wilderness for forty years. Not at all where we would imagine the best place to find **"Treasures of Darkness"**!

       Perhaps you are feeling as if you are in a wilderness situation and maybe you even think that the Lord has forgotten about you? Let this Scripture encourage you that the Holy Spirit is always working as the under-cover agent and at times, even if we can't see it, He is preparing us for the next stage of our journey towards our destiny! The Lord is often developing our spiritual hunger during those times. During this Lockdown period has become a wonderful opportunity to put the Lord firmly back in the centre of our lives and let go of all the "clutter" around us!!

BUT GOD turned up for Moses and He will for you too!!

       We read in Exodus 3:2-15 "The Angel of the Lord appeared to him in a flame of fire out of the midst of a bush, and he looked, and behold, the bush burned with fire yet was not consumed." **Moses had his unexpected ENCOUNTER with the Living God after 40 years!!!**, who says: "I have surely seen the affliction of my people who are in Egypt and have heard their cry because of their taskmasters and oppressors; for I know their sorrows and sufferings and trials. And I have come down to deliver them out of the power of the Egyptians and to bring them out of that land to a land good and large, flowing with milk and honey."...... "Come now I will send you to Pharaoh that you may bring forth my people out of Egypt.".

Moses experienced such **"Treasures of Darkness" in his encounter in the wilderness with THE Great I AM** ... YET... hearing that his mission was to go back to Egypt to deliver God's people must have been a bit of a shock to him! I am sure this was not at all what he wanted to hear!! How many times do we meet with the Lord and He says what we think we can't possibly manage, or we would rather not hear? This is when

God says... **"Now you are ready!"** It really is when we have no personal strength left that God knows that we are now ready to utterly depend on Him and Him alone! This has happened in my life so many times I have lost count!!!

One very good example was when the Holy Spirit asked me personally to host my own Conference for the very first time. I felt completely incapable of doing this! So, I went for counsel to a beautiful woman of God and confessed how inadequate I felt, and would she pray for me. The late Heather Double so graciously agreed, and this is what she prayed... "Lord, thank You for bringing Gill to an end of herself, increase her inadequacy and dependency on You as she steps out in this new venture. So now please Lord will you equip Gill with a new anointing of the Holy Spirit in power to do what you have asked her to do". This was not the prayer I was expecting... but I have learnt that it was exactly what I needed!!!

Moses must have felt like that... in his own eyes he thought he couldn't speak, he was afraid that the people wouldn't accept or believe him and, to cap it all... The Lord said He was going to make Pharaoh extra stubborn before he would let the people go! In answer to Moses' arguments, God chose to use what Moses had in his hand... a rod which was an ordinary shepherd's staff, to release the miracles in those days to convince the people that God had sent him. And also, ultimately, to demonstrate the most incredible miracles, in confronting Pharaoh who eventually did let God's people go but... only after all the first-born sons and livestock were killed as the angel of death passed over. The Lord also provided Aaron, his brother, to do the speaking for him and be alongside Moses.

The "Treasures of Darkness" were always there for Moses in this wilderness!

Time and time, as he led God's people out of Egypt... there were Miracles, Supernatural provision with the Manna, Water that came twice from the Rock, and even Quail to satisfy the disgruntled people of God who wanted meat. God provided EVERYTHING that they needed quite miraculously. Even their clothes did not wear out! Not to mention that God demonstrated His Power to all the people over and over again when the people questioned Moses' leadership. God appeared with His special Shekinah Glory resting on Moses, that the people might know that Moses was His chosen one even in the countless rebellions by the people.

45

Having re-read all the story of Moses, I am overcome by the way that the Lord God revealed His **"Treasures of Darkness"** to the most undeserving and rebellious people as well as to Moses... such was His loving kindness! The Presence of the Lord Himself was constantly abiding there with Moses, and God's people could actually see the Pillar of Cloud by day and the Pillar of Fire by night, not to mention the Glory that kept descending personally on Moses in the Tent of Meeting and the Tabernacle. Incredible difficulties were experienced in each step of Moses' journey. But through it all the Lord stood by Moses even when he made mistakes!

The Lord Himself was there all the time as the best Treasure possible!

So too with us, whenever He calls us, He will equip us with His Grace and Power in the Holy Spirit so that we can produce for Him much fruit that will bring Him tremendous Glory. I love it that later on in Numbers 12:3-7 when Aaron and Miriam challenge Moses' leadership... God actually says that Moses is the meekest, most humble man in all the earth... He calls Moses: "My servant Moses; he is entrusted and faithful in all My house". The Lord God must have developed such a close intimacy with Moses previously throughout all his wanderings in the desert for those forty years when he might have felt forgotten!

But NO! God is SO faithful and beautiful!

Listen, if you are obedient and faithful to the call of God... He will defend you, He will protect you, and He will be there for you always. That is His promise in 2 Timothy 2:11-13 "If we have died with Him, we shall live with Him. If we endure, we shall also reign with Him. If we deny and disown and reject Him, He will also deny and disown and reject us. If we are faithless He remains faithful, faithful to His Word and His righteous character, for He cannot deny Himself". Remember when He says in Isaiah 45:3 **"I will give you the Treasures of Darkness."** That is His Word for you and me!! We can stand on His Word always!

Chapter 8.

Treasures discovered in the Winepress for GIDEON!

When the Spirit of the Lord clothed **GIDEON**...

Judges 6:1-6, in the beginning of this incident in Israel's history, we see once again... "The Israelites did evil in the sight of the Lord and the Lord gave them into the hand of Midian for seven years". Because of this, God's people were full of fear and hid themselves in dens in the mountains as the Midianites, Amalekites and the people of the east came to destroy their crops, took their animals and livestock, and left them without nourishment. In today's language the whole economy was shut down and the economy was in great need!! A bit like the present Lockdown because of the Corona Virus!!

As I prayed, I saw the three distinct enemies that we all have to be aware of... The Midianites represent the World around us that causes us stress, pressures and burdens. While the Amalekites represent the Flesh that causes us to be unstable or vacillate as the dictionary says! Then there are the people of the east who can represent the Devil and are used by the enemy to sow seeds of destruction and darkness in our lives. Interestingly, the camels could not be counted as the Israelites were attacked! This, according to Biblical History, is the first time that camels were used as weapons! Apparently, the Midianites had the insight to use camels as an attacking force with the troops on foot and this terrified God's people! I suppose it must have seemed the same during the First World War when planes were first used, or missiles later on! New weapons create new fears, like this Virus! But every time that God's people suffered, whether it was their own fault or because of the enemy... what did they do?

Yes! The Bible tells us in Judges 6:6, "Israel was greatly impoverished because of the Midianites, and the Israelites cried to the Lord". How merciful is our God!! For seven years this misery had gone on and finally they decided to call out to the Lord for help! So like us, when we have been struggling in our own strength and finally we have no other answer... that is when we eventually decide to pray!! What a merciful Father He is! Oh, forgive us Lord! But it is often right then, in those times, that we are ready to...

"Dare to Receive the Treasures of Darkness!!"

Judges 6: 8-10 "The Lord sent a prophet" ... God reminded them that He had brought them up from Egypt out of the house of bondage and delivered them from the hand of the Egyptians and out of the hand of all who had oppressed them. Then God says: "I am the Lord your God; fear not the gods of the Amorites, in whose land you dwell. But you have not obeyed my voice.". The Prophet is speaking the truth that should always bring us to our knees in humility. But as so often happens... the people of God ignore the Prophet's voice! We would do well to remember that the word of the Prophet speaks truth and is sent to prepare the way for God's intervention!!

What treasures was God going to send this time?

In every darkness or difficult situation, whatever the distress when we cry out for help... In spite of our sins or foolishness... **GOD HEARS AND ANSWERS!** Isn't that just SO marvellous? But nearly always in whatever way the Word comes... the Spirit will remind us, like He did with the Israelites, what God has already done for us personally on the Cross. This should give us a new perspective and renewed vision enabling us to once again look for the hidden treasures we will find, instead of being confronted with our problems or difficulties that seem like huge mountains.

A change of focus helps us "Receive the Treasures of Darkness!"

For us, it is crucial that we remember and never forget all that our wonderful Saviour Jesus Christ has done for us on the Cross... that He **did** take all our punishment and **the penalty for our sins was paid in full** at Calvary. That He **has** born our sickness and **by His stripes we were healed!** Jesus **has** delivered us from the bondage we were in and **Jesus has forgiven us** and made us His own beloved children!! That **He has even given us the gift of Eternal Life** as we believe in the sacrifice of Christ Jesus at Calvary!! All of this is what has happened. **IF** we are Born Again and believe that Jesus' blood has washed away our sins, **THEN** we can respond once again to the mercy displayed at the Cross!

Now these treasures were not available to the people of God at this time... **BUT** here come the **"Treasures of Darkness for God's people"!** Judges 6:11-16... The Angel of the Lord appears to a young man called Gideon. He was afraid and is in the wrong place hiding from the enemy while he is trying to beat wheat in an underground winepress!! Crazy!!!

The only good thing was that he was not passive, but at least he was trying to do something in the bad situation! The appearance of the Angel of the Lord is what is called a "Christophany." In the Old Testament this is when Christ comes into the situation as the Angel of the Lord to bring a solution of redemption because He has heard the cries of His people.

Gideon is not expecting anything and yet the Angel of the Lord appears to him sitting under the Oak at Ophrah and actually initiates the conversation to him by saying: **"The Lord is with you, you mighty man of fearless courage"**. It is obvious that Gideon hasn't a clue who is speaking to him and he responds… "If the Lord is with us, **WHY** has all this befallen us? And **WHERE** are all His wondrous works of which our fathers told us, saying, did not the Lord bring us up from Egypt? But now the Lord has forsaken us and given us into the hand of Midian!" Oh dear! Gideon only sees the terrible darkness and a hopeless situation and doesn't realize that it is actually the Angel of the Lord that is speaking to him personally, not to all the Israelites.

I think that Gideon almost missed his encounter with the Lord!!

I can personally understand that so well… a few years ago as I was in a very tricky situation the night immediately prior to my big Conference, I was praying in the Spirit in bed, while Skippy, my husband, was asleep! I really didn't know how to resolve the problem or what message to give for the opening session at the Conference the following evening! Suddenly I knew that an enormous angel was in the far corner of the room! The atmosphere was electric and to my amazement I found myself asking the angel what his name was! Then even more incredible… he answered me!!! "My name is Sanctity I am sent from the Most High God to keep you holy and help you." Then he was gone! But heaven had deposited in those few seconds an amazing revelation and instructed me how to deal with the problem and given me a completely unique message that was just purely supernatural!! In my book, "Dare to Experience the Cross" there is a whole CHAPTER called "Secrets of the Cross" about my Grandmother's big brown handbag!!! Just a foretaste about what that means… The Holy Spirit showed me that my Grandmother's big brown handbag symbolized the Cross of our Lord Jesus Christ… SO many treasures hidden inside! Yes, and bit by bit the **"Treasures of Darkness"** are revealed as we visit the Cross again and again.

That encounter with the angel made me understand a little bit more how Gideon must have felt as he encountered the Angel of the

Lord!! Sometimes in these supernatural encounters it brings out hidden things from deep inside that we do not know are there! Every time we start questioning the Lord with our **WHY**..., we are in trouble and will come to a wrong conclusion just like Gideon. Why can be a sign of deep inner frustration and hopelessness, with our eyes firmly fixed on the problems and not on the Lord Who has the answer to all our problems! Similarly, if we ask **WHERE**..., we are in danger of digging an even greater hole for ourselves to fall into and an opening to believing the lies of the enemy.

Let's look at Gideon....

He has obviously heard the stories of how God had delivered His people in the past, but he is full of unbelief in his heart for the here and now! That can happen easily to us, when we remember that The Spirit of God has done wonderful things in the past and yet at that particular moment it seems as if He is a million miles away and unbelief begins to take hold of our minds. This is unbelief that is simply being deceived to believe the wrong things, and the Bible says in Hebrews 11:6 "Without faith it is impossible to please God". **Gideon comes to the wrong conclusion** and says: "Now the Lord has forsaken us and given us into the hand of Midian". It is a mixture of deception and truth which is never helpful to us. Yes, they were in the hand of Midian, but certainly the Lord had not forsaken them!

Now hear the Lord's reply... The Angel of the Lord ignores what Gideon has said and He goes on to commission him. "Go in this your might, and you shall save Israel from the hand of Midian. Have I not sent you?" It reminds me a bit of the commission that the Lord gave Moses!! Moses came up with all his arguments and now see that Gideon does the same! What happens is that the Lord is confronting Gideon in how he sees himself in a very negative way ... from the smallest clan of Manasseh and the least in his father's house. But the Lord simply says: "Surely I will be with you and you will smite the Midianites as one man". Here I believe Gideon's eyes are beginning to see above the circumstances and faith is starting to arise in his heart. He says: "If now I have found favour in your sight then show me a sign that it is You Who talks with me."

Gideon's response is ACTION... like many of us, he wants proof and yet he wants to do something to impress his Heavenly visitor, and asks him to wait while he prepares an offering of a special meal. In great poverty, Gideon goes over the top to bless the Lord. It must have taken some time to capture the kid, skin it, prepare it and roast it...plus making the unleavened cakes and the broth to go with the meal. That is Gideon's very best offering and then he hurries to bring it all, ready to eat...

BUT God is not looking for our offerings but our heart!

The Angel of the Lord responds and tells him to lay it all on a particular rock and then to pour the broth over it all... I can imagine Gideon's surprise and horror, especially as The Angel of the Lord then took His staff and touched the offering and fire came up from the rock and burnt it all up!! All Gideon's effort and expense... GONE in a puff of smoke!

THEN worse still, the Angel of the Lord disappeared!

Gideon had asked for a sign, and he certainly had one, but not what he expected!! It was in this moment that he must have realized that it had been the Lord... his eyes were opened, and a real godly fear came upon him and he thought he would die! Seeing his awesome fear, The Spirit of God then spoke peace to Gideon as he built an altar there to the Lord, and:

Gideon called it "Jehovah Shalom" ... The Lord is Peace.

This is the second revelation of God's Name we are privileged to see in the Word of God! This visitation continued into the night when Gideon was given specific instructions to pull down the altar to Baal that his father had set up and use his father's second bull and to cut down the Asherah pole next to it. Then he was to build an altar to the Lord on top of this stronghold and make a burnt offering. This must have been SO difficult!! Then we are told that Gideon took ten men of his servants to help him and they did it at night because he was too afraid to do it by day!

What is the lesson for us?

Be obedient to God's word and do it even if we are afraid!!

God will enable us! Blessings always follow obedience as I have said before! In the morning it must have seemed as if all hell broke loose... but amazingly Gideon's father stood up for him and he was not killed. Oh! This was such a close shave with death! But God rewards Gideon and his name is changed to Jerubbaal... one who cuts down!

So where, you might ask are "Treasures of Darkness"?

Oh, they are coming in Judges 6:33-34... believe it or not? After all this has happened, the Midianites and the other enemies started to gather and encamped against God's people in the Valley of Jezreel. In other words, it got worse!!

BUT GOD... The promise that the Angel of the Lord spoke to Gideon was fulfilled in the most supernatural and miraculous way! We are told in the Word of God that **"The Spirit of the Lord clothed Gideon with Himself and took possession of him,** and he blew a trumpet and all the clan of Abiezer was gathered to him." No greater **"Treasures of Darkness"** could ever have been imparted to Gideon! No wonder he went on to completely defeat all the Midianites. At first Gideon had 22,000 gathered to him but then God separated those who were afraid, and they turned back. That left 10,000; then only the ones who lapped the water with their hands were chosen... and only 300 remained! Judges 7:7 The Lord said to Gideon: "With these men I will deliver you and give the Midianites into your hand. Let all the others return every man to his house". God wanted to make sure that Gideon would never be able to say that he had defeated the enemy!!

God gave Gideon victorious "Treasures of Darkness" over the enemies.

The rest of the details of this incredible victory are there for you personally to read! After these great victories, the people wanted Gideon to rule over them, but Gideon said, "I will not rule over you, my son will not rule over you; **the Lord will rule over you"**. Out of this great darkness that was oppressing God's people for seven years, the Lord raised up a deliverer, Gideon, who really came from nowhere! He was God's chosen vessel to deliver God's chosen people so that all the Honour and Glory and Supernatural **"Treasures of Darkness"** were seen to come from God and not from man. Unfortunately, the story of Gideon didn't end so well, but we should never take away from the faithfulness of the Lord as He gave God's people peace in the land for forty years through Gideon.

I believe we are to be ready for Angelic visitations in these coming days that will change the circumstances and bring Heaven's intervention into our situations.

Never forget: God does His best work in darkness!!

The Holy Spirit is just looking for your availability!

Chapter 9.

Life-Changing Treasures out of Barrenness for HANNAH!

Here we see two women faced the same darkness, but circumstances were very different!

HANNAH and ELIZABETH!

The Bible says in Isaiah 54:1-5 "Sing, O barren woman, you who did not bear; break forth into singing and cry aloud, you who did not travail with child! For the spiritual children of the desolate one will be more than the children of the married wife" says the Lord. "Enlarge the place of your tent and let the curtains of your habitations be stretched out; spare not; lengthen your cords and strengthen your stakes. For you will spread abroad to the right hand and to the left; and your offspring will possess the nations make the desolate cities to be inhabited. Fear not, for you shall not be ashamed; neither be confounded and depressed, for you shall not be put to shame. For, you shall forget the shame of your youth, and you shall not remember the reproach of your widowhood anymore. For your Maker is your husband... The Lord of Hosts is His Name..."

It is important to realize in the context of these times... barrenness was considered a curse because children were seen as a blessing from God. Therefore, barrenness was viewed as a judgement from God for the woman's sin or the sins of
her ancestors in the past. In those days a closed womb was therefore a shameful condition and an unbearable stigma for a woman to carry. Of course, barrenness can mean so many different things to different people, like lacking an intimate relationship with the Lord, or lacking friends, or being alone without a family to support you. It can be living without a job or a dry time in ministry... and many other ways you can feel barren. Essentially, barrenness is simply not being fruitful!

BUT GOD makes the difference!!!

To most of us what God says here to the barren woman would seem really difficult for her... She is told to: Sing, Burst into song, Shout for joy and then to enlarge your place...in other words...get ready for the offspring!! Our counsel, I am sure, would be very different!!

So, I was wondering how it is that God sees so completely differently to us... I realized that I certainly needed new revelation in this and to learn from the Holy Spirit! All at once The Spirit opened up the Word to me and I understood! The Lord reminded me that **GOD IS "I AM" ... He is NOW**... He sees everything from completion because He is outside time... He has no tomorrow and no yesterday ... **every day is TO-DAY for Him!** No wonder Romans 4:17 says: "God calls things that are not, as though they were," because from His perspective He sees what was, what is, and what is coming because **He IS GOD!!**

The Lord is outside time!

So we are going to look and see what we can learn from **HANNAH** in the Bible... 1 Samuel 1:1-18... We see that God's people were living in the time of the Judges, some were good and some not so good, but the Lord God wanted a man to bring about the transition from the years of the Judges to a Monarchy. Again, the Lord is seeing far ahead and has **"Treasures of Darkness" all prepared and stored up for Hannah in her particular darkness!**

There was a man called Elkanah, his name means: God is Zealous and full of Zeal; and he has two wives: Hannah, meaning Grace and Favour; and the other, Peninnah, meaning Gloating Wizard. Peninnah has many sons and daughters while Hannah has none. Barrenness is a particularly dark emotional time as I have said, causing huge psychological and emotional baggage.

Remember darkness can be what we are lacking ...it can be the ABSENCE of something that is SO painful and heart breaking, bringing with it such darkness!

Elkanah dearly loved Hannah and gave her extra portions of food to try and make up for her barrenness; but she was crying inside and her heart was aching, which was such deep sorrow and it was made worse by Peninnah who provoked her year after year because she was childless. This was a prolonged agony of darkness!

Each year they would go to worship at Shiloh and this sorrowful woman Hannah went into the temple. On this occasion... there Eli the Priest, saw Hannah praying and we read... "she was in distress of soul, praying to the Lord and weeping bitterly". So, she made a vow from the depth of her anguish. "O Lord of Hosts… if you will indeed look upon the terrible affliction of your handmaid and remember and not forget your handmaid but will give me a son, I will give him back to the Lord all his life". Hannah continued praying in her heart and Eli the Priest thought she was drunk. She responded, "No my Lord, I am a woman of a sorrowful spirit… I was pouring out my heart before the Lord. Regard not your handmaid as a wicked woman; for out of my great complaint and bitter provocation I have been speaking". The Priest Eli said: **"Go in peace, and may the God of Israel grant your petition which you have asked of Him."** Hannah said, "Let your handmaid find grace in your sight." So, we read that she went on her way and ate some food and her countenance was no longer sad.

Something changed for Hannah that day!

In her darkness a simple prayer by the priest deposited a seed of faith and we are told she went and worshipped before the Lord before going home. When they got home, Elkanah her husband had intimacy with his wife Hannah and the Lord remembered her and she became pregnant and had a son Samuel whose name means: Heard of God!

Sometimes, for us to become fruitful, all we need is a re-connection with the Lord Himself as Hannah did in the Temple that day. By pouring out our heart to the Lord in agony of spirit and many tears with all the pain and darkness overflowing from deep within… barrenness is released, and an enabling happens so that she can truly give everything to Him. In this way she is unlocking the barrenness within us and opening herself to receive that seed of faith in her spiritual womb.

Nothing on the outside had changed for Hannah, but The Holy Spirit had lifted her eyes back on to the Lord Himself who is the source of all she ever needed! So it is with us… "Letting Go" is essential if we are to be free from the cancer of barrenness and be released into fruitfulness in whatever area we need.

What a wonderful "Treasure of Darkness!"

But more than that, God would now have a man devoted to Him, and that is what Samuel became! He served the Lord faithfully all His life as Priest, Prophet and Judge… he held the position as Judge and became the last of the Judges to rule God's people. Initially, he was used to anoint Saul to be king and then finally much later… Samuel anointed David to be king in place of Saul, and David became known as a man after God's own heart. Hannah's darkness and barrenness produced a precious treasure for Hannah, but more than that... there was a legacy of treasure for God Himself and for God's own people!

Don't be surprised at the "Treasures of Darkness" that God may have already planned for you!!

<u>There is always a much bigger picture!</u>

I was very aware of this when in June 2019 I was asked to pray for a young couple who had been trying for a baby for several years without success. They were really upset, and Hannah especially felt that she had failed her husband. Both of them now saw that the Lord was their only hope... It was one of those meetings when the Holy Spirit's Presence was SO powerfully rich, and people were experiencing release from all sorts of bondage, and many healings were taking place, and especially many young people were getting right with God... the atmosphere was one where faith was rising for miracles and they were just happening all over the auditorium!

But in that moment, when I was asked to pray, I honestly felt no particular word of faith... Except the power of agreement! I remember saying: "I will stand with you as you both come into complete agreement that barrenness will leave you Hannah and that the Lord will breathe His Life-giving Spirit into your womb and reverse the condition of barrenness, making you fruitful to the honour and glory of His Name.... and you will both welcome your baby". With that I laid my hand on her womb and commanded fruitfulness in Jesus Name!! Then I left the couple with a hug and said let me know when you are pregnant!! It was a simple prayer that sowed a seed of faith that the Holy Spirit was able to activate on their behalf!

Well, the glorious end of that story was that Hannah and Mike are now enjoying their little daughter, Amelia... God did the miracle almost straight away and I just praise and glorify the Lord that that couple are experiencing their little treasure and every day they are full of thankfulness to the Lord Himself!

Chapter 10.

More Hidden Treasures for ELIZABETH!

Now let's look at the other barren woman...**ELIZABETH**...Luke 1:1-25

There are similarities in that both women were barren and only God could redeem the hopeless situations. Both were loved by their husbands and both were godly women who were both experiencing having to come to terms with the reproach of their barrenness and the heartache it caused after many years.

With Hannah's circumstances, it was Hannah herself who initiated her encounter with the Lord by going to the temple at Shiloh and pouring out her heart and the Priest Eli praying for her... **BUT** with Elizabeth it was her husband Zachariah who had the encounter as he was serving in his priestly capacity in the temple, so it wasn't Elizabeth! Both Elizabeth and Zachariah were righteous in the sight of God and walked in a pleasing way according to all the commandments of the Lord. It had fallen by lot to Zachariah to enter the sanctuary of the Lord to burn incense... while all the people were praying outside. This special privilege probably only happened once in the lifetime of a priest and it was going to be marked with great treasure!

The name Zachariah means Yahweh remembers! I want to say that whatever your heartache... God remembers you and He cares for you and shares your pain. But even more wonderful than that is that The Holy Spirit has the supernatural power and desire to bring **"Treasures of Darkness"** into your life in the midst of heartache. In whatever you are lacking, the Lord is your provider. You may not be barren without a child, but in whatever emptiness and lack you are experiencing, the Lord will meet with you and satisfy the deepest longings of your heart.

If I can share personally, Skippy and I could not have our own children when we got married. I found this extremely difficult because when you love someone this is a heartache. Having said that... we have been truly blessed with a wonderful daughter Meryl and our son Cefyn from my first marriage. And so as the years went by and I was radically saved... the Lord Himself took away all that pain and it was not something I ever thought about, I was healed from the inside out! However, the Lord does not forget and many years later an amazing thing happened to me!

Once again, it was at the Good News Crusade Summer Camp where we were leaders and it happened to be the last night when Derek Prince, the brilliant Bible Teacher, was speaking. Skippy was looking after the children on the Campsite, so I was able to go to the meeting. Everyone felt for Skippy as he would miss the final night, to which he gladly replied, "Oh Gill will take wonderful notes, I won't miss anything!" Well, normally that is absolutely true, BUT it was the end of a very busy week and I was exhausted!

As a leader, I was sitting on the front row and began to try and take notes as Derek was speaking... I just couldn't! Sleep and tiredness swamped me, and I had to pinch myself to prevent myself from falling off the chair!!! I just couldn't get up and leave the meeting when such a distinguished speaker was in full flow!!! Suddenly I realized people were standing up! Thankfully I got up too, only to discover that it wasn't the end of the meeting but Derek was praying: "Now you barren women put your hand on your womb and I will release fruitfulness for you to have the child you long for!!" Oh, my embarrassment... I was long passed child-bearing age and without a womb after my hysterectomy!! But I stood there as dear Derek prayed and then I rushed out of the tent to disappear, totally embarrassed!

I am sure you too are smiling now as you read this, aren't you? Yes, there was much laughter as I recalled what had happened to everyone and tried to explain to those who were inquiring about why I had stood up to be prayed for so that I could have a child!! It took some explanations and good fun as you can guess! ... **BUT** do you know God did something really surprising that night and ever since He has given me many, many spiritual sons and daughters all over the world and I am SO blessed with every single precious one of them.

God NEVER forgets and He will remember you like He surprised me!!

Back to **ELIZABETH**... unbeknown to her, Zachariah was going to have an encounter to change everything and make a huge difference her whole life!! Zachariah was in the temple sanctuary when the Angel of the Lord came and stood right there at the right side of the altar of incense in the Holy Place in the Temple. We are told he was afraid because...

The Angel of the Lord said to him, "Do not be afraid, Zachariah, because your petition was heard, and your wife Elizabeth will bear you a son and you must call him John. You will have joy and delight, and many will rejoice over his birth. He will be great in the sight of the Lord. And he must drink no wine nor strong drink, and he will be filled with the Holy Spirit even in his mother's womb. He will turn back and cause to return many of the sons of Israel to the Lord their God. And he will go before Him in the spirit and power of Elijah, to turn back the hearts of the fathers to the children, and the disobedient and incredulous to the wisdom of the upright… in order to make ready for the Lord a people prepared in spirit, adjusted and placed in the right moral state."

Zachariah answers the Angel by questioning…

How can he believe what the Angel is saying is true, since he is an old man and his wife is old too? Doubting God's messenger is not a good idea! So NOW the Angel of the Lord reveals that he is Gabriel, who stands in the very Presence of God and he has been sent from God to bring this good news to Zachariah… BUT because of his unbelief in what Gabriel has said, Zachariah is struck dumb and will be silent until these things have come to pass at the appointed time! I do not believe that Zachariah was struck dumb as a punishment, but to prevent him speaking out doubt and unbelief that could prevent the miracle of Isaac coming to pass! Proverbs 18:21 "Death and Life are in the power of the tongue!

What an ENCOUNTER… the people waiting outside were wondering why he was spending such a long time in the sanctuary. However, when Zachariah came out unable to speak, they realized he must have seen a vision! In The Holy Presence of God's Angel, Gabriel, the supernatural had occurred for Zachariah and we are told he returned to his own home a different man and Elizabeth became pregnant! How did Elizabeth feel I wonder? It was not her who had had the word from God or the personal encounter.

But miraculously it was Elizabeth who "Received the Treasures of Darkness"!

Even as her husband was unable to communicate in words, yet he was still able to be intimate with his wife! Luke 1:24-25 says, "Now after this his wife Elizabeth became pregnant, and for 5 months she secluded herself entirely, saying, because thus the Lord has dealt with me in the days when He deigned to look on me to take away my reproach among men".

Do you know there are times when the Lord reveals something so special to us that we have to keep it hidden deep inside pondering just what has taken place and this can be real wisdom!! But there will come a time when it is right to be brought into the light! For Elizabeth, the baby was growing, and it must have been obvious that she was carrying a child… God's timing is so different to ours, but His timing is perfect. We are told in the Word of God that, six months after this, the same Angel Gabriel appeared to the Virgin Mary and the Holy Spirit overshadowed her and she was told that she would have a baby who would be called the Son of God! Gabriel also told Mary that her relative Elizabeth had conceived a son in her old age and that this was the sixth month with her that was called barren.

"For with God nothing is ever impossible and no word from God shall ever
be without power or impossible of fulfilment."

To which Mary responded, "Behold, I am the handmaid of the Lord; let it be according to what you have said". And Mary immediately arose and went to the home of Zachariah and greeted Elizabeth. It was at that exact moment as Elizabeth heard Mary's greeting that the baby leaped in her womb and Elizabeth was filled with the Holy Spirit! There was such joy that Elizabeth cried out with a loud cry… "Blessed above all women are you! And blessed is the fruit of your womb. And how have I deserved this honour to me that, the mother of my Lord should come to me? For behold, the instant the sound of your greeting reached my ears, the baby in my womb leaped for joy".

Can you imagine the exuberant joy that these two women experienced… the Holy Spirit was moving so powerfully that there was revelation and prophecy and overflowing praise of the sheer wonder of what the Lord God had done for them both!! Each woman rejoicing in the God of their salvation and remembering His faithfulness throughout the generations! **WOW! WOW! WOW!** They hadn't even seen the treasures yet, but they knew….

"Treasures of Darkness" were on the way!!

This really shows me that we need to **"Receive the Treasures of Darkness"** by faith because the Lord is the faithful God Who always fulfils His Word! And Yes! Elizabeth gave birth to a son at the appointed time and when they asked Zachariah what he was to be called he wrote on a tablet, "His name is John!"

At once his mouth was opened and his tongue loosed and Zachariah began to speak blessing and praising and thanking God. We are told that he was filled with the Holy Spirit and prophesied about the coming Messiah and then turned to his little son saying, "And you little one shall be called a prophet of the Most High; for you shall go on before the face of the Lord to make ready His ways. To bring the knowledge of salvation to His people in forgiveness and remission of their sins... a Light from on high will dawn upon us and visit us to shine upon and give light to those who sit in darkness and in the shadow of death, to direct and guide our feet in a straight line into the way of peace."

What AMAZING "Treasures of Darkness"

It was prophesied that those who sit in darkness will see the **GREAT LIGHT Himself**... Jesus is the Light of the world, and whatever darkness may be enveloping you right now; He promises that there is emotional healing, unlimited blessings and overflowing riches of the secret places for you. Just **COME** to Him, **COME** to Jesus! He is waiting to meet with you there in His Holy Presence. **COME** just as you are empty or hurting, dry or grieving, weeping or sobbing, ill or sick, angry or bitter... whatever... **COME** with your own heart cry like Hannah. Or perhaps you will **COME**, like Zachariah, on behalf of someone else that needs those treasures. The Holy Spirit will hear, and He will answer you and bring you through from any area of barrenness, and He will be so creative and surprise you with much fruitfulness that will bring much glory to God. I have been there, and I understand! But as the song says, Our God is The Way-Maker, Miracle-Worker, Promise-Keeper and **LIGHT in the DARKNESS**... that is Who He is!!

Believe that you will "Receive the Treasures of Darkness" at the appointed time.

Chapter 11

DAVID Waited Patiently for his Treasures!

DAVID... must be one of our favourites in the Bible, every child has heard about David killing Goliath! But as I was thinking about **"Treasures of Darkness"** I really saw him with a different revelation and understanding. David had to WAIT a long time to receive his treasures! **Maybe you too are in that waiting time?** It is not easy... but we can learn SO much from David's journey from shepherd boy to king of Israel. **Let's ask the Holy Spirit to guide us!**

1 Samuel 16: 1-3 "The Lord said to Samuel, how long will you mourn for Saul seeing I have rejected him from reigning over Israel? Fill your horn with oil; I will send you to Jesse in Bethlehem for I have provided for myself a king among his sons."

If you know the story, you will know that Samuel was very reluctant, as he was afraid that if Saul heard about this then he would be killed! However, the Lord takes no notice of his objections but tells Samuel how to do it. The Word says: v 3-4 "Invite Jesse to the sacrifice and I will show you what you shall do; and you will anoint for me the one I name to you. And Samuel did what the Lord said and came to Bethlehem".

We are told that Jesse presented all seven of his sons before Samuel... but not one of them was the one that God had chosen and so the Lord says: v7 "Look not on his appearance or at the height of his stature... for the Lord sees not as man sees; for a man looks on the outward appearance, but the Lord looks on the heart". Samuel had to ask specifically if there was another son and he is told that the youngest son, David, is out in the field tending his father's sheep! He wasn't even invited to the feast!

So here we see that David was overlooked as a youngster in the family, he was rejected as a son and not even considered to be anointed and it would appear that David was just being used to look after his father's sheep. It looked as if he was about to be forgotten because of where he was... outside the area of blessing!

BUT GOD! The Holy Spirit knew exactly where David was

and made sure he did not lose out!! How true it is as it is written in 1 Corinthians 1:27-29 "God deliberately chooses what the world considers is foolish to put the wise to shame and what the world calls weak to put the strong to shame. And God also deliberately selected what in the world is lowborn and insignificant and branded and treated with contempt, even the things that are nothing so that He might bring to nothing the things that are so that no mortal man can boast in the presence of God".

God chose DAVID! And He chooses you....

Often the world can have overlooked you and you might feel rejected and forgotten or given no value in your family or workplace or wherever... **BUT GOD** the Holy Spirit knows precisely where you and what has happened in your life. He looks at your heart and He chooses you!! On the Cross, in all His suffering, the Lord had you on His mind and saw you as His own special treasure!

There is a hidden potential in you that God sees even if you feel the pain like a great darkness heavily weighing upon you as you look back on your time of growing up in a dysfunctional family. The Lord had a plan for David, and He has a plan for you too."

Come on! Believe it!!

God had gifted David with several special talents and the particular gift to play skilfully on the lyre... this gift brought him before King Saul to get rid of the evil spirit that was tormenting him. So, for you and me it is important that we let the Holy Spirit show us our gifts and allow Him, in whatever way He chooses, to develop those gifts while we are in the process of waiting!

I am reminded that many years ago I was in that process of waiting as God had sent me back from Heaven to specifically preach the Word of God boldly and bring inspiration to people. Every door was firmly closed... it was a really difficult time! So, I started out as a Methodist Lay Preacher and I am really grateful for the input I had during that time, which gave me the opportunity of studying the Bible. But it was the work that the Holy Spirit was doing in me that was the most important thing which at the time I did not recognise!!

It took years of waiting and there were many times that I felt SO frustrated and I would weep before the Lord and wonder when my release would come. Those were really dark times and literally years went by and I am forever thankful that one dear lady gave me the opportunity to preach to several little fellowship groups of elderly ladies every Wednesday afternoon in some of the small churches around Wolverhampton. Oh, I cannot tell you how my gift was developed during those precious afternoons and how much I learnt of how to connect with all sorts of people from many different backgrounds.

Darkness proved to be my excellent training ground!

David must have felt a little like that! But then his big opportunity came in defeating the giant Goliath; it must have seemed as if Heaven was rewarding him with great treasures and a wonderful friendship with Jonathan, the King's son. However, it didn't last long, as David discovered that as the people praised him, Saul became very angry, envious and jealous of him; and led to David having to flee for his life.

It must be realized that Samuel had already anointed David to be king. **YET**... here he finds himself for the next few years running away from Saul's army that was trying to kill him. We do not know exactly how long David was pursued by Saul, but it must have been a very dark and difficult time for him. The only people with him at this time in the wilderness were about six hundred disgruntled, rebellious men following him! He had lost his wife, and everything must have seemed really dark... YET twice David had the opportunity to kill Saul, but he was proved faithful in not touching God's anointed.

Both times... once in 1 Samuel 22:1-2, **In the darkness of the cave of Adullam**, David cut off a piece of Saul's robe and could have killed him... but we are told that his heart smote him and even Saul agreed that David was more righteous than he was. Then again in 1 Samuel 26:7, **In the dark of night**, David and Abishai went into the enemy's camp, but Saul and all his three thousand men knew nothing because we are told that **God had put a deep sleep of darkness upon them.** David took the spear and a bottle of water from just beside Saul's head... but he couldn't kill him!

The journey in those wilderness years must have been immensely hard for David as he waited for God to deal with Saul. I am sure he was wondering if he would ever be king. Negative thoughts must have bombarded his mind! Even when the Philistines attacked Israel and both Saul and Jonathan were killed on the same day... David still honoured

Saul. I have noticed that all the time David inquired of the Lord... "Should I go after them?" Time and time again he didn't know what to do during this waiting time... but he continually obeyed the Spirit of God Who would instruct him in every instance.

Finally, after the death of Saul, David inquired again of the Lord: "Should I go up into the cities of Judah? Which city shall I go to?" And the Lord said: "To Hebron." It was there that the men of Judah actually anointed David king over the house of Judah. This was the second anointing for David!

At last, after all the waiting and traumatic years of being hunted and persecuted, David **"Received the Treasures of Darkness"**. Although it actually took another seven and a half years before he was eventually anointed king over all Israel. We read in 2 Samuel 5:1-4, it was then that all the tribes of Israel came to David in Hebron and said; "Behold, we are your bone and your flesh... The Lord told you, you shall feed My people and be prince over them". So, the elders of Israel came to the king in Hebron, and King David made a covenant with them there before the Lord, and they anointed him King over Israel.

David a man after God's own heart!

This was the third anointing and David was thirty years old when he began his forty-year reign. The Lord truly developed David during all those WAITING years! It was during those stretchy years that David wrote SO many Psalms during this difficult period of his life. But now we are the ones so blessed to **"Receive the Treasures of Darkness"** of the Psalms from David; and God's plan did prevail.

I want to finish this CHAPTER with a Psalm David wrote while he was running away; he was alone, no friend and perhaps at the lowest point in his life. As you read, see the anguish, hear the pain and see the treasures that David knows he has now received.

It's a journey of WAITING and afterwards the glory of Treasures Received!

Psalm 61:1-8 Passion Translation...

O God, hear my prayer. Listen to my hearts cry.
For no matter where I am, even when I am far from home,

I will cry out to you for a father's help.
When I am feeble and overwhelmed by life,
Guide me into your glory, where I am safe and sheltered.
Lord, you are a paradise of protection to me,
You lift me high above the fray.
None of my foes can touch me
when I'm held firmly in your wrap-around presence!
Keep me in this glory,
Let me live continually under your splendid-shadow,
hiding my life in you forever.
You have heard my sweet resolutions
to love and serve you, for I am your beloved.
And you have given me an inheritance of rich treasures,
which you give to all your lovers.
You treat me like a king, giving me a full and abundant life,
years and years of reigning.
Like many generations rolled into one.
I will live enthroned with you forever!
Guard me, O God, with your unending, unfailing love.
Let me live my days walking in grace and truth before you.
And my praises will fill the heavens forever,
fulfilling my vow to make every day a love gift to you!

      I cannot think of a better way to pray for you! So, this Psalm is my prayer for you in your **WAITING** time! Draw near and deeply fellowship with Father's heart, He will enrich you and faithfully guide you into His **"Treasures of Darkness"**. Yes! The ones He has reserved for you!! Take time to speak aloud each line of David's Psalm and pray it in with thanksgiving and make it personal. Be sure to open up, then the Holy Spirit will be able to do a tremendous work of amazing grace in your heart, healing you, helping you, and squeezing your heart to be finely tuned to His eternal purposes.

YES! The Spirit of all Power and Might will work as the
Supernatural
God to prepare you during this time of waiting so you will be able
to
REIGN in HIM!!

Chapter 12.

Treasures along the Way for ELIJAH!

ELIJAH... was born in Gilead, in the little town of Tishbe.

For many years Israel had been rotting in serious moral and spiritual decay and by the time Elijah had reached adulthood, they had come to an all-time low... you could say Israel was at the bottom of the pit! The golden age of David and Solomon was finished, and six other kings had come and gone in just 58 years... now the seventh king was worse than any of the others.

He was King Ahab, who did more to provoke the Lord than all the kings before! Together with his wicked wife Jezebel they had built up a full-time staff of 450 Baal prophets, plus an extra team of 400 prophets who served the goddess Asherah. Among the terrible Baal cult practices were child sacrifices that took a new-born baby from its mother's breast and it was thrown into the blazing furnace as the mother watched screaming... absolutely hideous! One thought comes to my mind that in these very days that we live in, there is a similar scream from the thousands of aborted babies and maybe it can be likened to the naked slaughter of the innocent in those days of Ahab... God have mercy!

Such darkness, and it covered the land!

So, we have the wicked King Ahab and his evil wife Queen Jezebel... enemies of God and God's people... working in ruthless co-operation with Satan. And we have, God's Prophet Elijah... he would have known the law from Deuteronomy 11:13-17 which says, "Do not let yourselves be led away from Yahweh to serve other gods. If you do, Yahweh will become angry with you. He will hold back the rain, and your ground will become too dry for crops to grow".

Could it be that the Spirit quickened that phrase to Elijah? "Hold back the rain."

I don't know, we are not told and neither do I know how, or in what particular way, the Lord spoke and commissioned Elijah to be His prophet... but what I do know is that... he did have the Word of the Lord!!

Elijah faithfully gave the Word of the Lord to King Ahab in 1 Kings 17:1 "As the Lord, the God of Israel lives, whom I serve, there will be neither dew nor rain in the next few years except at my word".

It is all very well to have the Word of the Lord... but we must be ready, willing and obedient no matter what the cost! God's Word took Elijah from nowhere to standing before this terrible King Ahab; and we see that God's Word gave Elijah incredible authority and supernatural boldness and gave him entrance before the King.

What supernatural courage he must have had!!

Before we go on from here, I would like to relate a true story that happened on a Mission Trip to Uganda. I was taking with me a young woman called Julie, as part of the team. It was her very first visit to Uganda. On the flight over, she casually said she had had a dream that there was oil to be found in Uganda. I honestly didn't take a lot of notice UNTIL the next morning! As we were having breakfast, we suddenly heard coming out of the live God TV a loud and clear and excited voice saying: "Great jubilation! Uganda is celebrating that oil has been found in the land!"

We were absolutely astounded as we all looked at Julie, who calmly proceeded to tell us that she had had another dream that night! This time she said she had a message for the President!! This was the essence of her dream!

That IF the President of Uganda used the oil wisely and shared the profits with the ordinary people of Uganda and he repented for all the previous corruption... then God would show them where there was gold in the land! Needless to say, we all prayed together and then we all went off individually to the different churches where we were due to preach that Sunday morning.

Remember, Julie had never even been to Uganda before and certainly she had never been to this particular church where she was preaching! As she came to the end of her message, she felt led to share her dreams about the oil and the message for the President publicly. Now it just so happened that for the first time ever the Born-Again Minister of Ethics had decided to come to that church that particular morning!! After the service, he rushed up to Julie and spoke urgently to her and said he would arrange the very next day for her to give this message to the President! He felt it was that important!!

ONLY GOD COULD HAVE DONE THAT!!!!

To cut a long story short, the next day, as a Team, we were all ushered into the main Government Ministerial Hall waiting for the President to arrive! It was a long day as the President was delayed, so Julie ended up dictating The Word of the Lord while another team member was typing it out to be given to the President! The result was amazing... the President proceeded to call a week of Prayer and Fasting for the whole nation ending up with a very large gathering in the National Mandela Stadium in Kampala where he publicly repented and re-dedicated the country back to the Lord Jesus Christ!!!

I am telling you this true story to illustrate just how powerful God's Prophetic Word is and that it will always carry such an anointing and will produce what it is sent to do! Can you see now how incredible it was that Elijah, from nowhere, should have an audience with this wicked King Ahab!

Darkness was prevailing in the land, but God's Word brought judgement...
and everything changed, opening the way for God's miraculous intervention!

However, for Elijah there was an unexpected repercussion!! He was personally in great danger and had to get away very fast! The word of the Lord came to Elijah saying, "Go from here and turn east and hide yourself by the brook Cherith east of the Jordan. You shall drink of the brook and I have commanded the ravens to feed you **THERE**". These were very specific instructions to Elijah, not at all what he would have chosen I am sure!!!

In the drought and famine and in the hard and difficult times... God is always provider, but Elijah has to be obedient and go to the particular place.

It is THERE that we find "The Treasures of Darkness."

Elijah, after he had been obedient and moved quickly and had hidden himself according to the word of the Lord; we see two sources of provision:

1.   The Natural brook with water to quench his thirst...**GREAT!**

2. The Supernatural provision of the ravens bringing bread & flesh meat every morning and evening...**OH NO!**

We all love the natural provision **BUT** how about the regurgitated food coming from the most unclean of birds???? Perhaps it's a wakeup call to us all that we need to be ready to **"Receive Treasures of Darkness"** in whatever way the Lord chooses to supply our need!! I believe Elijah made the most of things and possibly even got used to the strange provision after a while!

The thing is that God never wants us to be dependent on things or get too comfy, complacent or take His supernatural provision for granted! The Spirit of God wants us, always, to be utterly dependent on Him and ready to move on in the new season and to give up the old wineskins and let Him shape us and prepare us to be the New Wineskins for the New Wine and more glorious fruitfulness for our God. But sometimes we are not so willing to leave the familiar behind...

Yes! Elijah is just like us... the Bible tells us in James 5:17 "Elijah was a human being with a nature such as we have with feelings, and affections, and a constitution like ours; and he prayed earnestly for it not to rain, and no rain fell on the earth for three years and six months".

So, I guess Elijah needed a bit of a shove to move on!!

We read in: 1 Kings 17:7-9 "After a while the brook dried up because there was no rain in the land, and the word of the Lord came to him, Arise, go to Zarephath, which belongs to Sidon, and dwell there. Behold, I have commanded a widow there to provide for you".

Elijah must have felt as if it was his fault because of the word he had spoken! Now the brook was drying up because there is no rain and the supply from the ravens has stopped! But I have a feeling that Elijah would have remembered that God, who had already provided for him at the brook Cherith was the same God now and would have some provision all planned out for him whatever the circumstances!

The word "Arise" is an urgent command that Elijah has to obey immediately! The problem is that Elijah would probably have known that going to Zarephath will mean going into **God's Smelting Furnace,** as this is what the name Zarephath means! Also, it was 73 miles away across the desert!!! These were testing times of darkness for Elijah ... and to make

71

it worse Zarephath was only about 8 miles from Jezebel's hometown!!

Can you imagine how Elijah must have felt!!?

I tell you, there are times, my dear precious friend, when what God tells us to do will stretch us to the very limit of our faith walk. To be obedient can be very costly! Elijah would have needed to keep reminding himself that God is faithful and true to His Word!

My own experience illustrates this perfectly! It was New Year's Day, several years ago, when one of the young men in the Church had a terrible accident as his anorak hood blew over his face as he was cycling to Church. The result was he went full speed ahead into the rear of the car right in front of him. Miraculously a doctor was in the car behind and administered first aid, but Stephen was critically injured and taken by helicopter to Swansea Hospital from Aberystwyth.

As I was praying on the next morning for Stephen, the Holy Spirit spoke to me, "Go immediately and lay hands on him and I will heal him". Then I heard the Holy Spirit speak to me from Scripture… "The Son of Righteousness will rise with healing in His wings." I was a relatively new Christian at the time and had no idea where that Scripture came from until I looked it up and found it was in Malachi 4: 2!!! Now I had a dilemma, what should I do? I was meant to be working that day in the University where I worked? So, I rang my boss, who wasn't a Christian, I told him about Stephen and what the Lord had asked me to do!! I honestly thought he would say, no you must come into work… but to my astonishment he gave me the go ahead to do down to Swansea.

The first hurdle was out of the way, but I was scared and the whole drive down to Swansea I was praying in the Spirit! I came to the hill overlooking the town; I stopped the car and prayed with great earnestness, I can tell you! Because it suddenly dawned on me that Stephen was in intensive care… how would I get in? I need not have worried as I got to the door of the ICU when Stephen's mother came out and said, "Oh Gill, great that you are here, could you stay with Steve while I get a drink?"

So, in I went and saw Stephen all wired up and ready for an operation on his jaw. He had lost all his teeth… the point of contact with the car could have been that his head would have been severed or if it had been higher up, he would have been completely blinded. Now it was crucial that they operated immediately that morning to re-align his jaw bones. My heart was thumping... then I suddenly saw on the bed beside Stephen his Bible was open and although he could not speak, he pointed to a verse. YES! It was the exact same one that the Holy Spirit had given me that morning as I prayed... "The Son of Righteousness will rise with healing in His wings".

Now I knew that God had indeed sent me to lay hands on dear Stephen, so I quickly put my hands on his head and prayed in the Spirit over him and OFF I went!!! Later, I discovered that when they took Stephen down for the operation there was no need to re-align the jaw bones they were perfectly knitted together... ALL Glory to the Lord Jesus!

The reason I felt to share this was because I know how uncomfortable I felt that day as nothing like this had ever happened to me before! I desperately wanted to be obedient, but I had to do it afraid!!! Maybe you have experienced something similar or you held back when you know you should have done what the Spirit was telling you... Speak to the Lord right now and ask for His forgiveness and forgive yourself and then ask for another opportunity!!

God will find a way of giving to you....
"The Treasures of Darkness" you missed before!!

YES! We need to remember that God is always faithful even when we do not know what lies ahead; we must keep moving on by faith in God's Word and trusting His faithful character and not deviating from the path ahead. Walking by faith and not by sight can be an adventure through the darkness and trials along the way... so we need to keep in the forefront of our minds that there will...

"Treasures of Darkness" waiting for us when we get THERE!!

But hallelujah Elijah made it to Zarephath! He came through the difficulties of the 5-6-day journey across the desert and eventually came to **THE GATE** of the city. It is **THERE** that it is traditionally a **PLACE of BREAKTHROUGH**... and it is **THERE** that the thirsty Elijah sees a widow. She is obviously very needy as she is gathering sticks and he must have wondered whether she was the one God had commanded to provide for him?

The Bible tells us in: 1Kings 17:10-16 He called to her, "Bring me a little water in a vessel that I may drink." We are told that as she was just going to get it, Elijah called to her again and said, "Bring me a morsel of bread in your hand." This revealed her limitations and her desperate situation as she responded, "I have not a loaf baked but only a handful of meal in a jar and a little oil in the bottle. See, I am gathering two sticks, that I may go in and bake it for me and my son that we may eat it and die!" Two desperate people, Elijah and the widow… they don't know it, but they need each other so that God can be glorified and perform miracles of provision for them both…

It is a DIVINE CONNECTION THERE in Zarephath!

Shall we see how the Spirit of God is working?

Elijah is the more confident, so he says: "Fear Not, go and do as you have said, but make it into a little cake, then first of all bring it to me, and afterward prepare some for yourself and your son. For thus says the Lord, the God of Israel: "The jar of meal shall not waste away or the bottle of oil fail until the day that the Lord sends rain on the earth." She did as Elijah said, and she and he and her household ate for many days. The jar of meal was not spent nor did the bottle of oil fail, according to the word which the Lord spoke through Elijah".

The result was that they both enjoyed the supernatural provisions of **"Treasures of Darkness"**… the widow saw God multiply the little she had, and also Elijah was provided for according to the word that the Lord had spoken to him.

As we have seen before, there are times when the enemy comes to steal, kill and destroy and here he comes again… all at once the son of the widow becomes very sick and he died. This tragedy has a way of revealing that the widow has a deep hidden problem and even after many days of blessing, she turns and blames Elijah that he has come to call her sin to remembrance and kill her son.

What sin? We are not told!

Sudden trauma in our lives can make us come to wrong conclusions too and cause us to speak in too much haste out of past pain, hurts, anxieties, difficulties or even hidden sins. Elijah doesn't rebuke her but says: **"Give me your son"** And he took him from her bosom and carried him up into his own bedroom chamber.

There and then a very strange and unexpected thing happens ...

1 Kings 17:20-23... Elijah, man of God, and Prophet cried out and appears to blame God too! He said, "O Lord my God have you brought further calamity upon the widow with whom I sojourn, by slaying her son?" Then we are told that he stretched himself upon the child three times and cried to the Lord... "O Lord my God, I pray you will let this child's soul come back into him". And the Lord heard the voice of Elijah and the soul of the child came back into him and he was revived.

Elijah took the child and brought him down out of the bedroom and gave him back to his mother; and Elijah said, **"See, your son is alive!"** To which the widow said, "By this I know that you are a man of God and that the word of the Lord is in your mouth".

It is worth us remembering that if there is any root of bitterness or sin hidden inside us, the Holy Spirit will use any circumstances to reveal it! Obviously, even though the widow had seen and experienced for many days the supernatural provision of the meal and the oil not failing, she still had issues that prevented her from fully trusting that Elijah was indeed who he said he was!

In other words, the darkness of the situation had blinded her to being able to
"Receive the Treasures of Darkness."

This can happen to us too... so we need to make sure that we give everything into God's hands! Whatever has appeared to have died in our lives needs the Special Life-Giving Spirit of God to breathe afresh upon us once again THEN the resurrection life of Jesus can bring LIFE out of the darkness of death. It might be a dream, a relationship or a ministry... or even that PROMISE that hasn't yet been fulfilled.

WE NEED to "LET GO" just like the widow!

In our hands and in our hearts, things will remain dead....

BUT if we choose to Let Go and Completely Surrender

God is the only One who can bring anything back from the dead...

THEN I Promise you...

"Resurrection Treasures of Darkness" will come back into your life.

Chapter 13.

Good Choices bring lasting Treasures to RUTH!

Ruth 1:1-2, it was in the days when the Judges ruled, there was a severe famine in the land of Judah, and we are told that there was a certain man called Elimelech from Bethlehem in Judah who went to live in Moab. Pressures of the famine led him to make a very bad decision not just for him, but for his whole family! Moab was a land of idolatry, incest, a war zone and, worse than anything, Moab was under God's curse for ten generations. But Hallelujah... The Word says in Galatians 3:13 "Christ purchased our freedom, redeeming us from the curse of the Law and its condemnation by Himself becoming a curse for us. For it is written in Scriptures Deut. 21:23... Cursed is everyone who hangs on a tree and is crucified".

JESUS took every curse upon Himself...What a TREASURE!!

But it should still be real wake up call to all of us as we read about Elimelech, to be very careful that we do not make bad or hasty choices just because of our circumstances or emotions. If we do, it is inevitable that those fleshly choices will not only affect us but our families and other people too!

Elimelech should have known better, his name means God is King... Naomi, his wife's name means pleasant and contented, and they were living in Bethlehem, meaning house of bread in the land of Judah, meaning praise! They had been blessed with two sons: Mahlon, meaning joy, and Chillion, meaning song! The whole family dwelt in the place of God's blessings; they were God's chosen people in God's land... **BUT** the pressures of the famine in the land had turned Elimelech's heart to move away from God and make a bad choice to leave where they were blessed and go to Moab; and his decision did affect all of them, as we will see!

A bad choice will always have consequences!

The whole family lost the Presence of God, they lost the Protection of God, and they lost the Provision of God... and entered into the most terrible darkness.

First of all, Naomi's husband died. Romans 8:6 says, "The mind of the flesh which is sense and reason **without the Holy Spirit is death**, a death that comprises all the miseries arising from sin, both here and hereafter!" So, we can clearly see that an ungodly choice opens the door for the enemy to come and kill, steal and destroy. Satan came and stole the life of Elimelech.

When they arrived in the land of Moab everything changed for them... the two sons Mahlon, meaning joy, was now called INVALID; and Chillion's name changed from song to PINING! It is obvious to see the downward slippery slope that was happening in their lives! When this happens, once again, the devil, the prince of darkness walks into their lives playing on their minds, with the grief of losing their father, and seeing their mother as a widow without any support... so both sons now make really wrong choices too! Hopelessness, loss and heartache are symptoms that attract darkness as well as the increased pressures of needing provision, and the emptiness inside influences them to take wives from the women of Moab... Orpah and Ruth. The sons should have known better from the laws of Moses that it was forbidden for God's people to marry foreign women.

DARKNESS appears to have blinded them from doing what is right!

YET... Several years went by before disaster struck again... this time there was even more tragedy, death and more darkness and despair, as both the sons died. This now has left three grieving widows... Naomi, Orpah and Ruth. It is easy to see how their combined grief and sorrow drew these three women together. Naomi had not only lost her husband, but now she had lost her two sons as well. Darkness and heartache must have seemed as if it were swallowing them up with no way out...

BUT GOD! How could it be possible for the Lord to reach into these lives and turn them around so that they would "Receive Treasures of Darkness?"

Let's find out!!

Ruth 1:6... We read that, "Naomi arose with her daughters-in-law to return from the country of Moab because she had heard how the Lord had visited His people in giving them food in Bethlehem". Oh, this is SO exciting, that no matter how far away anyone might have drifted or in what terrible darkness they might be dwelling... God, the Holy Spirit, knows how to let us hear something that is going to turn around our lives! Hunger is a very strong motivator and these women would have been desperate for food!

Naomi HEARD that the Lord had visited His people in giving them food in Bethlehem.

I am sure that Naomi even in her sorrow was able to remember how good it had been in all those years gone past when they lived in Bethlehem. She would have remembered when they had God's Presence, His Protection and His Provision. Those treasures are always priceless, and the Holy Spirit quickens our spirit-man deep inside us to yearn for the Presence of God once again... as He did for Naomi to make her want to: **ARISE!**

Hallelujah! She made a momentous decision to return; and more than that, she acted on her decision and began to go on the way to return to Judah! In pain, all three widows made a good choice to leave Moab. Heartache had certainly united these three women as they all started on the way to Judah together. As my Skippy would say: It's not how you start that counts but how you finish!! So true!!

BUT in the tragedy of such a loss, we need to realize that Naomi was a wounded and grieving woman deep inside; and although she had turned around herself and was now going in the right direction, somehow or other she just couldn't see how Orpah and Ruth could go with her and leave their families when there was no hope of either of them getting a husband. This personal choice of Naomi's to return to Bethlehem had in a way brought both Orpah and Ruth to a crisis point... now they had to make their own choices.

We always have to make our own choices to... "Receive the Treasures of darkness!"

In the Kingdom of God, the Lord always gives everyone "free will"... it is His gift to us to be able to choose His ways or the ways of the flesh that lead to death. How we use this freedom of choice will result in blessing or curse!? However, whatever our choices, be assured that His everlasting love for each one of us will never vary... though we need to know that His presence can be forfeited!

We read in Ruth 1:9-10... that Naomi blessed her daughters-in-law who she greatly appreciated and then she urged them again to go back to Moab. "The Lord grant that you may find a home and rest, each in the house of her husband!" Then she kissed them, and they all wept aloud. And they said, "No, we will return with you to your people".

Orpah and Ruth again made really good choices, but still Naomi wasn't convinced; and she continued to try and persuade them again and again to go back to their land to their culture and their families... so they wept again and this time Orpah finally kissed her mother-in-law goodbye, but Ruth clung to her. Her name means: Forever Friendship!

Our good choices will be tested to see if we do really mean what we say!

Orpah, her name means: wild goat, stiff-necked, inflexible and unyielding. She chooses to go back to her land of Moab with idolatry, incest and conflict... and sadly she is never heard of again! Orpah had the opportunity for God's blessing but was persuaded to go back to what she was familiar with and chose to live under God's curse of darkness.

As I read that, I felt so sad... because Orpah ALMOST made it... but she missed out on the **"Treasures of Darkness"** because she did not stick to her good choices.

This should be a very clear warning to us!

BUT Ruth... Oh, she was SO different; in the face of Naomi's negative words and invitation to return to Moab... Ruth's heart was stirred up by the Holy Spirit to make the most amazing **Seven Choices that were Life-Changing Declarations** that would ultimately ensure that she experienced the **"Treasures of Darkness"** and fulfil her destiny that the Lord God had stored up and prepared for her!

Ruth 1: 16-17 Ruth said:

1) "Where you go... I WILL GO!" Ruth chose to die to her own will. If we are to **"Receive the Treasures of Darkness"** then yielding our will to   Father's will is imperative... Yes, just like Jesus did in Gethsemane when He faced the agony of the Cross and He said, "Not My will but Thy will be done." Ruth made an irreversible choice towards her destiny even though she didn't know how it

would work out. That is real trust and walking by faith!! We are all called to walk by faith and not by sight!

2) "Where you lodge...I WILL LODGE!" Ruth made a choice to dwell wherever Naomi would live. So too, for each one of us, it is important that we fully surrender where we are to dwell and identify with Christ as our dwelling place! It is THERE that we will experience all the blessings of our inheritance waiting for us! Make sure you know where your dwelling place is!!

3) "Your people... WILL BE MY PEOPLE" Ruth was now making a total commitment to leave behind everything from Moab. For us we need to be completely willing to leave our old life and follow Christ Jesus. In other words: Burn your bridges! This was a big decision for Ruth and ensured that she would indeed inherit the treasures waiting for her. In Christ we are a new creation and we are transferred and placed into a new family in the Kingdom of God...the old has gone and the new is here!

4) "Your God... WILL BE MY GOD." Now Ruth is not just committing herself to Naomi but to the Lord God Almighty Himself in a personal brand-new relationship. Ruth must have witnessed something in Naomi that she served the True and Living God and not the idols in Moab that Ruth had known before. In spite of Naomi considering herself a bitter woman because of everything that had happened... (we see that, because later she called herself Mara meaning bitterness), even so the light of her faith was still shining through! For all of us, we need reminding that when things may have occurred in our lives and we seem distant from the Lord or even actually backslidden... we must not underestimate the light of Christ in us that can be evident even in the darkest of times.

5) "Where you die... I WILL DIE." Ruth was saying in effect that nothing will be able to separate her from Naomi, not even death. What a wonderful way that is pointing to the Cross of Jesus our Lord and Saviour. There must come a time for all of us to die with Christ... Paul said in Galatians 2:20 "I have been crucified with Christ, it is no longer I that live, but Christ that lives in me, and the life that I now live I live by the faith of the Son of God Who loved me and gave Himself for me". Experiencing the Cross personally is crucial!

6) "Where you will be buried... I WILL BE BURIED." This follows on from the previous declaration and points to us being buried with Christ in baptism. Colossians 2:12 "You were buried with Him in your baptism in which you were also raised with Him to a new life through your faith in the working of God, as displayed when He raised Christ from the dead". If you haven't gone through the waters of Baptism, being fully immersed and not just sprinkled, then you will find it hard to understand the resurrection life where we "**Receive the Treasures of Darkness.**"

7) "Nothing but death... WILL PART ME FROM YOU." Ruth is looking beyond the here and now; she is fixing her eyes on eternity. We too need to make our choices with eternity in view because that is our real home! Here in this life we are just passing through, because we are destined to be enthroned in Christ Jesus our Lord as citizens of the Heavenly Kingdom above! Oh Glory, how wonderful that will be!!!

We cannot allow these incredible declarations by Ruth to pass us by without you and I making our personal response... Of course, we do not make these promises to anyone except the Lord Jesus Himself. So, I urge you to spend some time praying through each commitment. This is the way to live under the total Lordship of Jesus Christ and experience all the victories He won for us at Calvary. It is a life lived in the supernatural power of the Risen Lord Jesus as we yield completely to the Holy Spirit! I promise you that there is nothing to lose and everything to gain... for now and eternity as we are committed to pleasing the Father as Jesus did, we will receive ALL the hidden riches in the secret place! Hallelujah! These commitments will certainly produce real, lasting **"Treasures of Darkness"** as you fully surrender and take up your Cross and follow Jesus.

So, Naomi and Ruth proceed to go on together to Bethlehem at the time of the Barley harvest. Ruth asks permission from Naomi to glean in one of the fields and what she actually says turns out to be a prophetic word... Listen! Ruth 2:2 Ruth speaks to Naomi and says,

"Let me go to the field and glean among the ears of grain after him in whose sight I shall find favour."

Ruth certainly received the favour she spoke of as the Holy Spirit directly led her straight to the field that belonged to Boaz and he just happened to be the wealthy kinsman of Naomi's husband! Ruth has a very good reputation that goes before her and she certainly does find favour as she is given extra grain provided for her. Boaz tells her personally to stay in his fields where she will be safe and even invites her to share a meal with him.

Treasures are beginning to come to Ruth!

In Ruth 2:11-12 Boaz said to her, "I have been made fully aware of all you have done for your mother-in-law since the death of your husband, and how you left your father and mother and the land of your birth and have come to a people unknown to you before. The Lord recompense you for what you have done, and a full reward be given to you by the Lord, the God of Israel, under whose wings you have come to take refuge".

Little did Ruth know then that Boaz was indeed the Redeemer Kinsman and that he would eventually take her to be his wife and that they would have a son called Obed who was the father of Jesse, who later was the father of David, the ancestor of Jesus Christ!!

WOW! What an inheritance and legacy Ruth was about to receive!

Read in Ruth 3:1-12 It is such a beautiful way that Ruth is led to lie down at the feet of Boaz and she answers his question when he says, "Who are you?" And Ruth says, "I am Ruth your maidservant. Spread your wings of protection over your maidservant for you are a next of kin". And Boaz responds, "And now my daughter, fear not, I will do for you all you require, for all my people in the city know that you are a woman of strength, worth, bravery and capability. It is true I am your near kinsman".

Everything had been in complete darkness and hopelessness **BUT GOD**... the Holy Spirit was at work behind the scenes as Ruth honoured her mother-in-law Naomi and she made one honouring decision after another and kept making the good choices... All the time God was moving her closer to when miraculously He would make sure Ruth would **"Receive the Treasures of Darkness"**.

I think it's appropriate here to share another true story! Skippy and I were being welcomed and staying in a home in UK and our hosts asked us if we would like to see a documentary programme on TV? It turned out to be about the Silver Mines in Australia and suddenly the Holy Spirit whispered that He had something to teach me!

I watched intently, wondering what it could be... and all at once the commentator began to explain what happened in the 1800's. Apparently, when the silver was first discovered there was a big rush to get this treasure, almost like the American gold rush earlier! Many men left their jobs and families and homes to get the valuable silver hidden deep underground in the mines. Then, as I listened and watched the programme, my heart really dropped as it was announced that over 800 men lost their lives trying to get this treasure. The silver was there, the mines were open, and the men were willing to leave everything; they made all the right choices to get the treasure **BUT** in those days they didn't have the right breathing equipment and they suffocated and died for lack of oxygen. It wasn't until this last century that those mines were re-opened again after many years and today it is a thriving business as they produce most of the world's silver. It was then that the Holy Spirit's still small voice clearly spoke to me deep in my heart:

"Gill, make sure that you never go after My Treasures of Darkness in your own strength or without my anointing."

This is a very important message that we can clearly see and learn from the story of Ruth... she never went after fulfilling her own desires for a husband, a child or provision for herself. She simply saw something in Naomi and wanted to be with her and chose to serve and provide for her and ultimately serve the God that Naomi loved. And we certainly see that The Lord rewarded her! So with us, our motivation must be to: Walk daily with the Lord Jesus Christ, Follow Him wherever He leads, Honour Him and Serve Him faithfully all the days of our lives... Our reward will be from God and not from men!

"Dare to Receive the Treasures of Darkness"

Chapter 14.

Glimpses of Treasures from the Prophets....ISAIAH and JEREMIAH!

ISAIAH... Was a prophet to four kings of Israel and he grew up in the Kingdom of Judah; he was married and had a family, his sons were given symbolic names... Shear-jashub, meaning a remnant will return; and Maher-shalal-hash-baz, meaning swift to plunder and quick to spoil! These names carried messages of warning from God to the people of Judah who were responsible for introducing idolatry into the Jerusalem temple. Isaiah repeatedly warned his people that there would be judgement because of their wickedness, but at the same time he also offered assurance to those who trusted in God.

Constantly Isaiah had spoken out boldly against the evil practices of the day, but he always managed to show the people how to come back to the Lord and be in a right relationship with Him. Isaiah 1:16-19 says, "Wash yourselves, make yourselves clean; put away the evil of your doings from my eyes! Cease to do evil. Learn to do right! Seek justice, relieve the oppressed, and correct the oppressor. Defend the fatherless, plead for the widow. Come now, and let us reason together, says the Lord. Though your sins are like scarlet, they shall be as white as snow; though they are red like crimson, they shall be like wool. If you are willing and obedient, you shall eat the good of the land".

Isaiah, as a Prophet of God, saw ahead of time the ruin of Judah and Jerusalem but he also saw the supernatural spiritual revelation of the coming Messiah as the Branch of the Lord Who would come with the Spirit of burning to purge away all the filth of God's people. He prophesied that in the day when God's people ignored the Lord, there would come a great army from afar that would come against the Jews and bring them into captivity and that it would bring great darkness and distress. Isaiah felt God's pain and it was a very heavy darkness to him.

But because no one was listening to him!! Something had to change!!

Many times, the Holy Spirit works very deeply in us before we are ready and willing to **"Receive the Treasures of Darkness"**!! He needs to prepare us, and I am sure you can relate to that!? This is why the Lord explained to me that I needed a new revelation of darkness so I could understand better!

The key is hidden in Isaiah 6:1-9 "In the year that King Uzziah died, I saw the Lord sitting upon a throne, high and lifted up, and his train filled the most holy part of the temple. Above Him stood the seraphim; each had six wings; with two each covered his own face, and with two each covered his feet, and with two each flew. And one cried to another and said, Holy, holy, holy is the Lord of hosts; the whole earth is full of His glory! And the foundations of the thresholds shook at the voice of him who cried, and the house was filled with smoke. Then said I, Woe is me! I am undone and ruined, because I am a man of unclean lips, and I dwell in the midst of a people of unclean lips; for my eyes have seen the King, the Lord of hosts! Then flew one of the seraphim to me, having a live coal in his hand which he had taken from off the altar; and with it he touched my mouth and said, Behold, this has touched your lips; your iniquity and guilt are taken away, and your sin is completely atoned for and forgiven. Also I heard the voice of the Lord saying... whom shall I send? And who will go for us? Then I said: **"Here I am send me." And God said, "Go and tell this people."**

Suddenly I began to see the treasure!

Isaiah had been prophesying but without the specific call of God and the special anointing up till this point! Isaiah had experienced this amazing new encounter and now his life changed forever. All that he had been saying before was true as he spoke out all the "woes" and "judgements" to God's people... **BUT NOW Isaiah saw himself!! "Woe is me!"** A message always has to work IN us first before it carries the anointing that will impact others!!

Compassion is a GREAT treasure!

In the face of such a holy God everything has to change... that is when we are being radically prepared ready for a new anointing and God is the One Who has to send us and equip us into the new season. This is purely God's business! It is a truly humbling experience when you see your own uncleanness and your own ruin in the Presence of the Lord God Almighty. Isaiah has been prophesying to the people **YET NOW...** he sees his own unclean lips and realises he is no better than the people he has been judging. He sees the glory, hears the singing, and the angelic seraphim... and then there is the SHAKING from the very foundations as the voice of God cries out and smoke fills the house!

This happened to me many years ago when the Lord took me personally into a moving vision of Calvary and the Cross of Jesus Christ. It was as if **I was there** watching the flogging and seeing the cat of nine tails ripping Jesus' skin off His back; **I was there** as He stumbled under the weight of the Cross as He made His way up to Golgotha the place of the scull; **I was there** as the crowd cried out "Crucify" Him; and **I was there** as Jesus was nailed to the Cross. I saw the blood spurt out as the nails went in and I saw His shoulders dislocated as the Cross thumped into the ground. I cannot tell you how awful it was... far worse than the film of "The Passion"!! But even as I screamed out that He was innocent, nobody took any notice of me! Then **I was there** as the Centurion drew his sword to pierce Jesus and another terrible scream left my lips as the sword went into Jesus' side and I saw the blood and water pour out. **I was there, it was horrific**... then the Centurion turned around... but NO it wasn't the Centurion that I saw... **but I saw it was ME!** In my hand was the sword dripping with blood and at that moment the words came to me from the Father.

"That is what your adultery has done, it's killed My Son."

At that moment **right there**, my heart felt as if it was broken into a million pieces and there was only one cry rose from my mouth... **"Have Mercy! O Lord Have Mercy!"** Then I saw the Lord Jesus lift His head just a little and He spoke out... "Father forgive Gill, she didn't know what she was doing". But do you know it was Jesus' eyes of love as He looked at me that pierced my innermost being. At that same moment I literally felt the blood of Jesus, warm and sticky flowing all over my head and then down over my body and then cleansing deep inside me.

I was clean...Oh Hallelujah!

Oh, the thankfulness that gushed into my spirit and overflowed in praise and gratitude! That was the moment when the Lord of Glory filled me with His Spirit and gave me the supernatural Gift of Tongues! I had never heard about speaking in a love language, I had no idea what had happened but all I knew it was SO GOOD!! Especially as I listened to the Holy Spirit speaking to me personally and affirming His love for me and how precious I was!

Nothing is more wonderful to me than knowing that I am forgiven and cherished in spite of my terrible sins! This encounter was confirming my commissioning from the Lord Himself when He originally sent me back from Heaven to preach His Word and inspire His people! From that particular moment I learnt to recognise the sweet small voice of the Spirit and know what He was saying to me! It was from this incredible experience in my life that so many miracles started to happen in so many instances and affect other people.

Oh, my Beloved friend, you can never underestimate what God can do when we encounter the Cross of Jesus Christ and see our own sinfulness and His mercy triumphing over darkness!! It was life-changing for Isaiah and it can be the same for you. Read again what happened to Isaiah in his awesome vision... Isaiah receives the best treasure that could ever have come to him. His lips are touched with the fire of a coal off the altar in heaven and he hears the amazing words:

"Your iniquity and your guilt are taken away and your sin is completely atoned for and forgiven."

Isaiah could not experience the Cross, as we can now, but he had a deep foretaste of what was to come at Calvary for all mankind. No wonder he could write later about the suffering Servant as he did in Isaiah 53. He knew intimately what it was like to **"Receive the Treasures of Darkness"**. Isaiah learnt how to open his spiritual ears and listen in to Heaven's conversation between the Father, the Son and the Holy Spirit who were speaking in the Heavenly realm above! WOW! He became tuned into the Spirit dimension! That is what can happen to us as we experience the Cross personally! In this encounter Isaiah was personally transformed from the inside out and then sent out and commissioned.

"Go and tell." Oh Hallelujah!!

Of course, we cannot arrange such encounters, but we do need to be ready to respond with our whole hearts and be alert so that we shall not miss these special times! You see, these treasures are not for ourselves... but to enable us so that we can overflow in the anointing to bless others with the treasures that the Holy Spirit has graciously given to us.

Isaiah 43: 19 "Behold, I am doing a new thing! Now it springs forth; do you not perceive and know it and will you not give heed to it? I will even make a roadway in the wilderness and rivers in the desert."

Beloved! This Prophet of God has been there... Isaiah has experienced the darkness and found the treasures to give away! His words are as relevant today and they continue to speak to us... especially at this unprecedented time as we all come out of this Lockdown situation! Isaiah has many more treasures to share with us that came to him from the darkness of his own days. Search diligently and go treasure hunting with the Holy Spirit and He will reveal the hidden riches from the secret places in the Word of God. You will find that they will help to lead you into this new season confident that The Lord Himself goes before you and me!!

"Dare to Receive the Treasures of Darkness."

JEREMIAH... was born into a priestly clan and called to the prophetic ministry when he was just a youth. His call in Jeremiah 1:5-10 was very clear from the beginning. "Before I formed you in the womb I knew and approved of you as my chosen instrument and before you were born I separated and set you apart, consecrating you and I appointed you as a prophet to the nations." Then I said... "Ah Lord God! Behold, I cannot speak, for I am only a youth." But the Lord said to me... "Say not, I am only a youth; for you shall go to all I shall send you, and whatever I command you, you shall speak. Be not afraid of their faces for I am with you to deliver you." says the Lord. Then the Lord put forth His hand and touched my mouth, and the Lord said to me, "Behold, I have put my words in your mouth. See, I have this day appointed you to the oversight of the nations and of the kingdoms to root out and pull down, to destroy and to overthrow, to build and to plant."

Under the reign of King Josiah, Jeremiah was supported by the king and there was much revival in the land of Judah... these were the golden days when Jeremiah's ministry was highly respected. However, after King Josiah was killed Jeremiah went through SO many days of great darkness, numerous challenges of persecution and imprisonment, he was thrown into a dungeon, beaten, put in stocks, threatened and almost killed. Despite the opposition Jeremiah faced, he remained true to the messages God gave him and was known as the weeping prophet!

As I have read the book of Jeremiah I began to wonder...

Where would I find "The Treasures of Darkness?"

Then I began to realize that there was never a time when the Holy

Spirit was not there with Jeremiah in whatever darkness he experienced… The Spirit was always comforting and encouraging him. One of the passages really exemplifies this: Jeremiah 18:1-6 "The Word which came to Jeremiah from the Lord: "Arise and go down to the potter's house, and there I will cause you to hear my words." Then I went down to the potter's house, and behold, he was working at the wheel. And the vessel he was making from the clay was spoiled in the hand of the potter; so he made it over, reworking it into another vessel as it seemed good to the potter to make it. Then the word of the Lord came to me: "O house of Israel, can I not do with you as this potter does?" says the Lord? "Behold, as the clay is in the potter's hand, so are you in my hand, O house of Israel."

This is a crisis situation when Jeremiah had encouraged the people and he had also warned them repeatedly and faithfully spoken every word that the Lord has asked him to say… **YET** they would not listen! How disheartening for Jeremiah!!

BUT GOD!

What would the Lord do? The treasures always come from obedience… as Jeremiah goes down to the potter's house! The Spirit imparts something special to Jeremiah and faith arises in all the difficulties he is experiencing. In spite of the nation's rebellion and all that is dreadful and all that is happening in Jeremiah's personal life… that is not the end of the story! God opens his eyes to see beyond and understand that whatever is put into the hands of the Divine Potter can be re-moulded… yes, even a nation! The Lord goes on to say about the house of Israel… so you are in my hand. God has not given up on His people and He never will, even when it looks completely dark and hopeless.

Personally, I can identify with Jeremiah as I found myself in a really unexpected situation when people I loved and served believed a lie about me that I was homophobic and had been accusing someone in a service when I was preaching. The result was that I was brought into a court-like set up. It was completely unbeknown to me what was about to happen, and the accusations were fired at me. I was so staggered, to say the least, and I was just about to defend myself when the Holy spoke into my heart… "Gill do you want to be more like Jesus?" Immediately I knew my answer was yes! So, He said, "Be silent and say nothing!" I simply wept before all my accusers and said nothing! All they saw was a broken woman… but Father saw a child of God hurting and being treated unjustly and He drew me into His everlasting loving arms. Did they ever ask forgiveness? No! But

90

God's mercy flowed out to them as I was graced to forgive them from my heart and, amazingly, we are still very much my friends and we have sweet fellowship together!

Sometimes what happens in our lives brings **"Treasures of Darkness"** to us in unusual ways, as the Lord Himself ministers His Grace and Love in an extraordinarily precious way that changes us from the inside out.

In Jeremiah 31:3 The Lord speaks to him in such a beautiful way, The Lord appeared from of old to me, saying, **"Yes I have loved you with an everlasting love; therefore with loving-kindness have I drawn you and continued My faithfulness to you."**

WOW! Isn't that a fabulous treasure?

Perhaps you may be in a very difficult circumstance right now as you are reading this book and everything is looking black and hopeless… **BUT** the Lord has His own personal special **"Treasures of Darkness"** for you. It's the very best, it's HIMSELF with you and He will never leave you or forsake you and He has the power to change whatever we put in His hand! You may be weeping in your heart right now and feel completely alone like Jeremiah did too, but the Word of the Lord came to him and it will come to you too and open your eyes to see wonderful things that will lift you up close to His heart.

There are times when we do not see the answers we want but we can always invite the Person of the Holy Spirit to help us and comfort us!

HE HIMSELF IS OUR DEAREST TREASURE!

Chapter 15.

Treasures of Protection... DANIEL and his friends!

As we continue our treasure hunting with the Holy Spirit... There are times in our lives when the innocent get hurt and affected by the mistakes and crimes of other people. This was the case for young Daniel and his friends who were taken captive by the Babylonians when they captured Jerusalem and they then suffered a life-long exile in Babylon because of Judah's prolonged disobedience to God. They were captured and brought from Jerusalem into Babylon and trained for service in the Babylonian government; but they did not let their misfortune destroy their relationship with The Lord. Instead they continued to put their trust and faith in God with great courage and faced the realities of exile and yet lived successful lives.

Standing up to the pressures around us produces "Treasures of Darkness."

This portion of Scripture shows us how to deal with tragedy and challenging circumstances that we might encounter. The Bible says in Daniel 1:8-16 that Daniel and his friends refused to defile themselves by eating the rich portions of food and wine from the kings table. To do this, they had to stand up with great courage to the pressures of what was expected of them, but we are told that God made Daniel find favour, and after 10 days it was seen that he and his three friends were looking much better and had taken on more flesh than all the other youths who ate of the king's rich dainties! The result was that they were all promoted for their wisdom and assigned to stand before the king.

Daniel 3:10-18 Later on, however, Nebuchadnezzar, the king, made an image of gold and everyone was ordered, at the sound of the horn, to bow down and worship this golden image, with the ruling that whoever did not fall down and worship would be cast into the midst of a burning fiery furnace. The pressures were building on the three friends as they continued to refuse to bow down and they found themselves before a very angry King Nebuchadnezzar who tried to persuade them to change their minds saying, "Who is this God who can deliver you out of my hands?"

Courage and Boldness are Treasures!

Their Babylonian names were Shadrach, Meshack and Abednego and they replied… "If our God, whom we serve, is able to deliver us from the burning fiery furnace, He will deliver us out of your hand O King. But if not, let it be known to you, O King, that we will not serve your gods or worship the golden image." WOW! That is very courageous in the face of a furious King Nebuchadnezzar! Especially as he now orders the furnace to be heated up seven times hotter than usual.

This is a very real GREAT DARKNESS… what will God do?

Shadrach, Meshach and Abednego are then bound up with all their clothing on and fell face down into the burning fiery furnace… it was so hot that even the three men who handled them were burnt up and killed. **BUT GOD…** suddenly the King looked and was astounded as he saw four men walking loose in the midst of the fire! He says in: v25 "I see the form of a fourth man who is like a son of the gods." Then Nebuchadnezzar called to Shadrach, Meshach and Abednego you are the servants of the Most High God, "Come out and come here."

The Treasure of a Miracle!

Daniel 3:26-30 As they came out, we are told that everyone could see that the fire had no power upon their bodies, not a hair of their heads singed, neither were their garments scorched or changed in colour or condition, nor had even the smell of smoke clung to them. Then Nebuchadnezzar said, "Blessed be the God of Shadrach, Meshach and Abednego, who has sent His angel and delivered His servants who believed in Him!" And the King gave the three of them treasures as they were promoted in the province of Babylon.

Maybe this is a story you are very familiar with… but I wonder if you have seen the amazing protection of **"The Treasures of Darkness"**? They were in a foreign land; it could have seemed wise and easier to have compromised their faith in the God of Israel, but instead they risked their lives rather than deny their God. But as we have seen already, when God steps in, things change!! This reminds me of the ultimate darkness that Esther faced in order to save her people when she said, "If I perish, I perish!"

God loves us to step out in faith!

To me the only way to really experience the amazing protection of the Lord is to come to the very edge of the precipice! I suppose that is why the Holy Spirit called my ministry... The Cutting Edge! I decided right at the beginning when I met with the Lord Jesus Christ and I identified with His death on the Cross... as I have quoted before and will write it again... like Paul in Galatians 2:20 "I have been crucified with Christ, it is no longer I that live, but Christ that lives in me and the life I now live I live by faith in the Son of God who loved me and gave His life for me".

Supernatural protections are incredible **"Treasures of Darkness"** as the Holy Spirit intervenes when we put our whole faith and trust in God... what glorious adventure!! That is what is SO exciting about walking in the Spirit and not according to the flesh!

The Lord loves to surprise us!

God's protection for us is always a very real illustration of His **"Treasures of Darkness"** for us and we should never take our experiences for granted or belittle them even though they may not be quite like it was for these three young men!!

I remember, on one occasion that Skippy and I were travelling back from seeing our daughter in Sheffield University... we were singing and worshipping the Lord when all of a sudden, as I was overtaking on the outside lane of the M1, I was completely blinded! The bonnet of our car flew up and hit the windscreen! Immediately I yelled out loud... "JESUS Help!" Without being able to see anything, the Holy Spirit guided us safely into the nearside lane and I was able to stop! In the midst of many vehicles the Lord had protected us, and we were able to tie the bonnet down and continue the journey rejoicing that the God of our salvation had indeed given us His supernatural protection!!

As I have been thinking about all these **"Treasures of Darkness"** I am beginning to realize that there are probably many more times when the Lord has protected us and yet, it is probable, that we may have just forgotten how good He has been to us on numerous occasions! I think it may be the time to ask the Holy Spirit to remind us and reveal to us how wonderful His protection has been! We need to be thankful for the big instances and the small ones, as they all reflect the **"Treasures of His Protection"**.

The Book of Daniel has several illustrations of these "Treasures of Darkness"

Daniel 6:1-24 Here in this particular portion of scripture we can read the story that this time during the reign of King Darius, there was a plot against Daniel who was distinguished above all the other presidents who served the King. They couldn't find any occasion to find fault against him, except that he was known for praying to God. So, they manipulated the King into making a decree that anyone who prayed to any god during 30 days and not to the King... would be cast into the den of lions.

Daniel knew in the extreme darkness of this situation he was being set up to be destroyed! **BUT GOD**... Daniel went into his house, with his windows open toward Jerusalem, he got down on his knees three times a day and prayed and gave thanks before his God, as he had done previously. Daniel was not going to be intimidated as he put all his faith in the true and living God and carried on as usual!

Daniel was given supernatural faith!

Then three men came and found Daniel praying and making supplication before His God and they reported him to the King. We are told that the King was really distressed and tried to save Daniel, but the pressures prevailed... so the King commanded Daniel and he was brought and cast into the den of lions.

The King then said to Daniel, "May your God, whom you are serving continually deliver you!" Then Darius sealed the huge stone with his personal seal and spent the night fasting before rising early in the morning and going to the den of lions. He cried out in a loud voice of anguish... "O Daniel, Daniel servant of the living God is your God whom you serve continually, able to deliver you from the lions?"

Daniel answered... "O King live forever! My God has sent His angel and has shut the lions' mouths so that they have not hurt me, because I was found innocent and blameless before Him; and also before you, O King, I have done you no harm."

It appears that the king was exceedingly glad and Daniel was brought up from the den with no sign of any harm found on him because he believed and trusted in his God. But those who accused Daniel were thrown into the den of lions and eaten before their bodies reached the ground as they were overpowered by the lions.

"Treasures of Darkness" glorify God!

Wonderfully King Darius made a new decree that all his royal dominion must bow and tremble and fear the God of Daniel, for he said... "He is the living God and His Kingdom shall not be destroyed and His Dominion shall be even to the end of the world. He is Saviour and Deliverer, and He works signs and wonders in the heavens and on the earth... He has delivered Daniel from the power of the lions". So it was that Daniel prospered in the reign of Darius and later too in the reign of Cyrus.

Psalm 18: 11 "He makes darkness His hiding place."

Again, I see that having faith in our God involves acting on our beliefs and trusting Him when we cannot see a way out of the darkness! May we all be encouraged that we serve the same God as Daniel and He still has the power to keep us safe and deliver us from whatever we may encounter that has been planned against us by Satan. We need to remember there is always God's special heavenly protection for us as we trust in Him!

"Treasures of Darkness" are promised for us today.

I have been pondering about certain instances in my own life and realized that they are not nearly so dramatic!! But just as surely, the Lord has given me **"Treasures of Darkness of Protection"** ... Many years ago, I had gone to Prestatyn in North Wales where The Christian Conference called "Spring Harvest" was being held and booked a large mobile home for a group from the Church. I arrived ahead of the main party and went to get the keys from the owner's house.... No-one appeared to be there, so I went in through the gate... calling out, "Hello! Hello!" expecting the owner to appear! However, what appeared was not the owner but a ferocious German Shepherd Dog with his big white teeth showing as he growled at me and it was obvious that he was going to pounce at me almost immediately! In that instance, I knew I had two choices... Run or Stay????

Then the Holy Spirit came upon me and I looked directly into the dog's eyes and found myself saying, "I command you in the Name of Jesus Christ of Nazareth to be still and not attack me". It all happened SO quickly, but literally he stopped growling and turned around and walked quietly away from me back into the house!! Now I understand the dog was defending his owner's property and I was the intruder... **BUT GOD... protected me!!** Job 20: 26... "Every misfortune is laid up for

96

His treasures."

Psalm 57:1… "Be merciful and gracious to me O God… be merciful and gracious to me, for my soul takes refuge and finds shelter and confidence in You, yes! In the shadow of your wings will I take refuge and be confident until calamities and destructive storms have passed."

These are "Treasures of Darkness" for you!

CHAPTER 16.

God sent His Own Son into Darkness...
JESUS CHRIST!

John 3:16 **"For God so loved the world that He sent His only begotten Son into the world** that whoever believes in Him will not perish but have everlasting life."

Galatians 4:4-5 "In the fullness of time... **God sent His Son,** born of a woman, born subject to the regulations of the Law, to purchase our freedom."

John 1:4-5 "In Him (Christ) was Life and the Life was the Light of men. And the **Light shines on in the darkness, for the darkness has never overpowered it.**" John the Baptist declared that he was not the Light but that he had come to bear witness to the true Light which was Jesus Christ.

Philippians 2:6-7 Talking of Jesus Christ, Paul says, "Let Him be your example in humility: Who although being essentially one with God and in the form of God (possessing the fullness of the attributes which make God...God) did not think this equality with God was a thing to be eagerly grasped or attained, but He stripped Himself of all privileges and rightful dignity, so as to assume the guise of a servant in that:

He became like men and was born as a human being".

With the help of the Holy Spirit I want to unpack these Scriptures a little... Jesus said of Himself... "I am the Light of the world". John the Baptist said, of himself, he was not the Light, but he had come to bear witness to the True Light which is Jesus Christ! I began to realize, just in a very small way, what it must have been like for Jesus to come, as a human being, into the terrible darkness of the rebellious and idolatrous world. He even came into being within the darkness of His mother's womb, hidden away for nine months where He had to grow in the darkness, just like us and YET... He was the Light of the world!!

AMAZING!

Willingly He had left the Glorious God-Light of the Heavenly Realm and the Majesty of the Glory at His Father's side; He left The Throne and encountered such darkness as never before... all because He chose to bring Salvation to you and me! He always knew His purpose was to die, He always knew that the darkness would try to overcome Him and that He was called to bring LIGHT wherever He went. It must have been such an awesome experience for Jesus and YET knowing that He was called to bring light and fulfil the word that was prophesied in Isaiah 9:2 "The people who walked in darkness have seen a great Light; those who dwell in the land of intense darkness and in the shadow of death, upon them has the Light shined".

Jesus literally fulfilled this prophesy.

Then, as Jesus was about to begin His ministry, He directly spoke that particular Scripture that we see in Matthew 4:16 "The people who dwelt enveloped in darkness have seen a great Light, and for those who sat in the land and shadow of death... Light has dawned". Jesus came and fulfilled every single prophecy concerning what was prophesied about Him. Jesus came to dispel the darkness because in Him was no darkness!

HE IS THE GREAT LIGHT

In Isaiah 53:2 it tells us, "For the Servant of God grew up before Him like a tender plant like a root out of dry ground; He had no form or comeliness, that we should look at Him, and no beauty that we should desire Him. He was despised and forsaken by men, a Man of sorrows and pains, and acquainted with grief and sickness; and like one from whom men hid their faces He as despised and we did not appreciate His worth or have any esteem for Him."

That must have been great darkness!

The Son of God Himself, Jesus Christ, the Anointed One, the Messiah, the Promised One... He was from above yet He came into the utter darkness of our world to bring to us all the **"Treasures of Darkness"** like no one else could ever do!!! He understands... He has experienced every degree of darkness that can be imagined and much more! He knew what it was like to be falsely accused and He knew that some people would actually prefer the darkness and not want to come into the light. He experienced people wanting to kill Him, falsely accusing Him, push Him off a cliff and stone Him and ultimately crucify Him... **YET wherever**

He went He brought light into the darkness... Hallelujah, What a Saviour!

Acts 10:38... "God anointed and consecrated Jesus of Nazareth with the Holy Spirit and with strength and ability and power; how He went about doing good, and in particular, curing all who were harassed and oppressed by the power of the devil, for God was with Him". This is what he did everywhere He went to demonstrate...

Light is far more powerful than darkness!

I have tried to imagine how my Jesus managed to walk in such darkness and not be affected by it? My conclusion is that He was always completely enabled by the power of the Holy Spirit... because the Light that Jesus carried was so much greater than the darkness! I believe that Jesus was never affected by the darkness because He knew He was the Light and it dwelt in Him; Maybe that doesn't seem like any great revelation to you... but to me I am aware that as He lives in me then... if Jesus could do it, so can I, and so can you! It was also the extraordinary motivating love of God that moved Jesus with compassion to touch the leper, to heal the sick, to deliver the oppressed, and use the Holy Spirit's supernatural powers to glorify His Father in Heaven. I don't believe Jesus was restricted by the darkness at all because He continually walked in light!

Jesus, Himself, is God's Special Treasure for US!

This will enable us to walk as Jesus walked as it says in 1 John 2:6 "Whoever says he abides in Him ought (as a personal debt) to walk and conduct himself in the same way as Jesus walked and conducted Himself."

Such a challenge!!... YET we need to remember in 1 John 4:4 the Bible says, "He who lives in you is greater than he who is in the world." Jesus IN you and Jesus IN me is the Light of the world and always:

Light will always dispel the darkness!

So, for us to **"Dare to Receive the Treasures of Darkness"** we need to understand much more deeply just how Jesus dealt with the situations of such immense great darkness. Like the excruciating pain of Judas betraying Him, Peter denying Him, and then facing the agony of the Cross beforehand in Gethsemane. Everyone deserted Him and not to mention the horror of the actual three hours of physical darkness that Jesus experienced on the Cross when the Father and the Spirit had to turn away

100

because Jesus actually became sin as He personally took away our sins in His own body.

How did our Jesus manage!?

Hebrews 12:2 This Scripture will give us a glimpse... "He, (Jesus) for the joy of obtaining the prize that was set before Him, endured the cross, despising and ignoring the shame, and is now seated at the right hand of the throne of God.

Just think of Him....."

I believe that the **PRIZE,** or you can say, the **TREASURE** set before Him was you and me... and every person who believes in Jesus OR WILL ever come to believe in Him for Salvation... **WE are His Treasure!** Even when He was unable to move as he was nailed on the Cross, He thought of us: "Father forgive them for they know not what they do". His last drop of blood was poured out to cleanse us and give us His life... Jesus did not hold back anything but laid down His life willingly!

John 19:30 Literally, Jesus breathed out His last breath... He cried out, "It is finished!" And He bowed Hs head and gave up His spirit. Luke 23:46... Jesus crying out with a loud voice said, "Father, into your hands I commit my spirit! And with these words He expired". Jesus literally breathed out His life for you and me so that we could have the gift of Eternal life as we believe in Him!

That is EXTREEM LOVE in action! "Treasures of Darkness" for us!

God is LOVE... Jesus exhibited Father's Supernatural LOVE... and the darkness had to flee! I believe He was re-fuelled in this extraordinary love every day of His life so that He could go around doing everything that pleased The Father. He did not allow the darkness to infiltrate Him because He was SO filled with Light, Love and Mercy. Always, He only did what He saw the Father doing, and only spoke what the Father told Him to speak and how to say it! It is this wondrous love that paid the debt we could never pay, and that love has won my heart!!

Oh the glorious love of God streaming from Jesus even in the dark tomb where He was buried alone... where He would have experienced that total darkness, shut in and abandoned FOR US! The stone was not rolled

101

away for Jesus to rise from the dead. It was rolled away for us to see that He wasn't captured by the darkness and He could never be restrained in human burial garments.

Hallelujah!! HE IS ALIVE FOREVERMORE!!!!

The tomb of isolation was the last darkness that Jesus endured... and death could not hold Him!! He defeated the last enemy... the darkness of death has been defeated once and for all who believe in Him! Jesus did not raise Himself from the dead... No! It was God the Father and God the Holy Spirit Who lifted Him up from the grave and God is well able to lift you or me up from the difficulties of our situations as we remember that He has promised to give us...

"The Treasures of Darkness and hidden riches of secret places"

What Glory! What Celebrations! What Majesty! What Mystery! What Power was released at the Resurrection of Jesus Christ! All these treasures and blessings are for us who believe in Jesus Christ as our Personal Saviour... Choose Him today, Choose Life and Choose Light, Choose Jesus Christ, Choose Freedom! He is the One who gives us the Gift of Eternal Life!

"The Treasures of Darkness" are reserved for us in Heaven BUT they are
ours be experienced wonderfully by faith here on earth...
Hallelujah!

But for me, the very best, the most marvellous thing of all is that I can incredibly and actually personally **"Be His Treasure"**!!! Yes! Jesus saw me and he saw you as **"His Treasures of Darkness."** It cost Him everything... it cost Him His life and **YET** today, I know He smiles and says, "You were worth all the pain, you are My Special Treasure and I love you with an everlasting love that will never pass away.

That is what won my heart! Oh, how I love Him!!

Chapter 17.

Hidden Riches in Secret Places... The SEED!

John 12:24 "Unless a grain of wheat falls into the earth and dies, it remains just one grain; it never becomes more but lives by itself alone. But if it dies, it produces many others and yields a rich harvest."

Jesus Christ is recognised as **The Seed of God** and we realise that He did indeed fall into the earth and die for us... that enables Jesus to bring forth a great harvest! **We are indeed His treasure!** Romans 8: 29 says, "That He might become the firstborn of many brethren".

So, I have been pondering again and again with the Holy Spirit what the Word of God says about seeds! 1 Corinthians 15:36-38 "Every time you plant a seed, you sow something that does not come to life unless it dies first. Nor is the seed you sow then the body which it is going to have later, but it is a naked kernel, perhaps of wheat or some of the rest of the grains. But God gives to it the body that He plans and sees fit, and each kind of seed has a body of its own". Certainly Jesus' resurrection body was totally different and certainly He died and was buried... Jesus is THE Seed Who was sown in dishonour and yet raised in strength and endued with power! Sown a natural body and raised with a supernatural body!

My natural father was an excellent gardener and I recall when I was very small being given a small packet of seeds. My Dad had also given me a small patch of his big garden that was exclusively mine! I was excited when he got a little trowel for me and showed me how to make a small trench where I could plant the seeds one by one. However, like many small children I just tipped the whole packet into one spot and covered them over with the soil! I loved watering them every day with my little watering-can!! I can remember the anticipation each day going to see whether they were growing and because I was impatient, I would dig them up... not a good idea!! When eventually just a few of the seeds that were left in the earth began to sprout, I was excited to see marigolds and other flowers coming up... but I remember crying because I couldn't find where my seeds were; had they disappeared???? They had completely vanished! To me it is still a miracle that a little ordinary seed can turn into something so beautiful after it is sown in the darkness of the soil!

This is a secret transformation happening in the darkness!

Treasure is sure to spring up as the seed always grows towards the light! All it needs is good soil and water and no interference from an impatient child!!! I realize that that is how the Holy Spirit works in us as we are Born Again from the Incorruptible Seed of Christ that is sown in our hearts. He works the miracle of transformation deep inside us to make us into the image of Christ... from glory to Glory!! Isn't that wonderful? Yes! It is true that we do need to die to our own lives, our own desires and dreams and decide to live for Him... but our Father in Heaven is the perfect Gardener!! And He knows the harvest he is planning to produce in our lives!

Hallelujah!

Jesus spoke about seeds in Mark 4:3-8 "Behold a farmer went out to sow and as he was sowing, some seed fell along the path and the birds came and ate it up. Other seed fell on ground full of rocks, where it had not much soil; and at once it sprang up, because it had no depth of soil; and when the sun came up, it was scorched, because it had not taken root and it withered away. Other seed fell among thorn plants, and the thistles grew and pressed together and utterly chocked and suffocated it and it yielded no grain. And other seed fell into good well adapted soil and brought forth grain, growing up and increasing, and yielded up to thirty times as much, and sixty times as much, and even a hundred times as much as had been sown!"

The Disciples didn't understand, so they asked Jesus about this parable and He explained it to them in Mark 4: 14-20 "The farmer sows the Word. The ones along the path are those who have the Word sown in their hearts **BUT** when they hear, Satan comes at once and takes away the message which is sown in them. And in the same way the ones sown upon the stony ground are those who, when they hear the Word they at once receive and accept and welcome it with joy; **BUT** they have no real root in themselves, and so they endure for a little while; then when trouble or persecution arises on account of the Word, they are offended and they stumble and fall away. And the ones sown among the thorns are others who hear the Word **BUT** then the cares, and anxieties of the world and distractions of the age, and the pleasure and delight and false glamour and deceitfulness of riches, and the cravings and passionate desire for other things creep in and chock and suffocate the Word and it becomes fruitless. **BUT** those sown on the good soil are the ones who hear the Word and receive and accept and welcome it AND BEAR FRUIT... some thirty times as much as was sown, some sixty times as much and some a hundred times as much".

So... for us to **"The Receive the Treasures of Darkness"** there are several things we need to check about the soil of our hearts and then we can be sure that we will bring forth much fruit to glorify God when we learn from the Word of God!

"Dare to Receive the Treasures of Darkness"

What sort of soil is in our hearts?

1. **The Seed is the WORD of God**... it always has Truth, Life and Potential to produce a big harvest in us! It's the ground of our hearts that is the challenge...

2. **The PATH** is where the ground has been trodden down. Our hearts can become hard and calloused so that the seed of God's Word cannot penetrate. It is those hurts and wounds that have damaged and hardened our hearts, so we tend to put up barriers to prevent ourselves from getting hurt again! Often it happens in childhood or it can even unfortunately occur in the Church. When this happens, our hearts become hardened and that is when Satan comes and steals the Word of God that could have helped us and set us free!

    Let me give you an example: If you have been badly treated and rejected then that spirit of rejection can come in and take up residence in you and will reject others... that is the way Satan operates! A rejected person hardens their heart for fear that they will be rejected again. It is a self-preservation mechanism that leaves the seed of God's Word exposed so that it can easily be stolen. The truth of God's Word is Ephesians 1:7 "You have been accepted in the Beloved and been given the treasures of redemption by Christ's Blood". That is the Truth!! But if your heart is hardened, then instead of allowing that seed of the Word of God to bring forth fruit... it is snatched away by the devil. **The result is: NO Treasure for the Lord!**

3. **The STONY ground** is where our hearts are shallow and we are

not really rooted in the soil of God's marvellous love... The seed of God's Word is received with joy and seems to be doing well in our lives for a short while but because of troubles or difficulties we can get offended and the Word does not impact our lives in our actions, reactions or attitudes. It will appear as if we are repeating the same mistakes again and again instead of allowing the Word of God to change us from the inside out! It seems like we just can't trust the Word of God!

Let me give you an example of this: For instance, if you have been a very generous person and given a financial gift to someone, then you might discover that that person has squandered the money in a way you think is very unwise... it is possible that you could have taken offence? A wrong reaction could be: "That will be the last time I will bless them!" But the Word of God comes: Luke 6:38 "Forgive over and over and you will be forgiven over and over. Give generously and generous gifts will be given back to you, shaken down to make room for more. Abundant gifts will pour out upon you with such over-flowing measure that it will run over the top! Your measure of generosity becomes the measurement of you return". So immediately you receive the Word joyfully until the enemy makes sure that you remember what happened before... so you do nothing, and the Word of God does you no good. **The result is: NO Treasure for the Lord!**

4. **Among the THORNS** is where our hearts are divided and poisoned by other things that seem more important than pleasing The Father. The soil has not been cleared of the rubbish... so that the worries and anxieties of every day seem to crowd out the Word of God and there are distractions so that Jesus is not Lord of all. There are emotional passions that come in and choke and suffocate the life that is in the Word of God. The result is that the Word ceases to have any effect in our lives and we do not reflect the character of Christ choosing to ignore the Word of God and instead going our own way and not following Jesus.

    Let me give you an example: Maybe you have been asking the Lord to provide you with a husband (or a wife) and you meet a really nice young man (or woman) who is not a Christian. Physical emotions run high and when the Word of God comes in: 2 Corinthians 2:14-15 "Do not be unequally yoked with an unbeliever do not make mismatched alliances... for what partnership is there between righteousness and rebellion? Who could mingle light and darkness? What harmony can there be between Christ and Satan? Or what does a believer have in common with an unbeliever? What friendship does God's temple have with demons?" The seed of God's Word is choked and strangled by your own passions and you ignore the Truth! **The result is: NO treasure for the Lord!**

5.   **The GOOD SOIL** is where our hearts have been softened and tenderised by the love of Christ. This is where we welcome every single Word of God and are responsive and teachable to the Holy Spirit, even when our flesh wants to pull in the opposite direction!! We make good choices to please the Father. This good soil eagerly receives the good Seed of God's Word. How much we cherish and allow the Word to grow and direct our lives will depend on how much Harvest we will produce… some thirty, some sixty and some a hundred times as much as is sown! **The result is: treasure for the Lord!**

Planting seeds and Burying sometimes can look the same!

In planting seeds, you dig a hole and place the seeds into the darkness of the soil, cover it over, and then WAIT in faith… There is always an expectation that the planted seeds will be transformed into something beautiful, and that happens in the secret place of the darkness of the earth! Eventually, those seeds will sprout because there is that hidden potential of life in the seed! That was my experience as a small child in my Daddy's garden!

However, when you bury something you also dig a hole, a bigger hole usually, then you also cover it over with soil… But that is the difference, there is no expectation of new life! Both are similar… yet very different! I asked the Holy Spirit to reveal a new way of looking at these two instances. This is what He shared with me:

Sowing!

In our lives God plants the seeds of Christ's character into our spirit-man from the moment we are "Born Again" … then the Holy Spirit waters those seeds deep in the secret places of our lives. The Bible says in Galatians 5:22 "The fruit of the Spirit is the work of His Presence within us and accomplishes: love, joy, peace, patience, kindness, goodness, faithfulness, gentleness and self-control."

I am sure, like me, you have found that these seeds of the fruit of the Holy Spirit take time to develop deep inside us! We would all love for these fruits to arrive fully flourishing in our lives right from the beginning... but that is not the way that the transformation happens. It is little by little in the secret depths of our being that these fruits begin to sprout! But the potential is promised in the seed that has been planted... it is an incorruptible seed... and given the right conditions these seeds will spring forth and manifest in our lives to the glory of God. These are beautiful and unlimited **"Treasures of Darkness"** that come in seed form and develop and produce fruit as we respond and yield completely to the Holy Spirit.

Burying!

Now when we bury something, at one level, there seems to be no treasures... UNTIL the Lord showed me that in Burial there needs to be a **"Letting Go!"** There are things in our lives that need to be buried and not dug up time and time again! Resurrection occurs when we truly release these things and leave them behind! Jesus demonstrated this when He was buried... He left behind the grave clothes and was resurrected with a new body!

Let me explain... The truth is that on the Day of Salvation all our **SINS** have been washed away in the blood of Jesus Christ shed at the Cross two thousand years ago! Hallelujah! We are told that the Lord does not remember them as they have been put as far away as the east is from the west or in the deepest sea! However, the enemy wants us to keep digging them up, feeling the shame and guilt of the past instead of "Letting them Go!" If the Lord doesn't remind us of our sins, then neither must the enemy be allowed to dig up what has been buried!

Another way the enemy tries to keep us digging up things that need to be buried once and for all are: **REGRETS!** These should not be allowed to surface as they need to stay buried because we cannot alter our past! When we know with eternal certainty that we have been forgiven at the Cross... it is an affront to deny the work of Calvary by allowing regrets to surface again and affect our present lives with condemnation. "Let them Go!" When they remain buried then the Lord is able to bring resurrection transformation into those situations and actually, later on, He can use them for His Glory, and they become **"Treasures of Darkness"**!

At times in our lives we can take **OFFENCE** and it is crucial that we need to make things right with whoever has offended us. It is even possible to be offended with God because He might not have seemed to answer our prayers in the way we desired! Whatever the offence... put it right and then bury it and "Let it Go!"

Fear comes from the kingdom of darkness because 2 Timothy 1:7 says, "God has not given us a spirit of fear but a spirit of love and power and a sound mind". **ALL FEARS** need to be buried in the soil of God's love because 1 John 4:18 says, "There is no fear in love, dread does not exist, but full-grown love turns fear out of doors and expels every trace of terror! **Perfect love casts out all fear!**" The enemy will try to bring fears back into our lives, but if they have been buried in the soil of the love of God then they can have no further hold on our lives.

So, my beloved friend... planting seeds points to a potential rich harvest for the Kingdom of God so that we can bear fruit for the Lord and for others... our reward is stored up in Heaven! How it happens is a mystery of transformation in the hidden places of darkness. Now is the time and opportunity to decide and pray that you will become a prolific planter of seeds in other people's lives!! Because the Lord has been SO generous in planting all those seeds in you and me... we must not waste one single seed of the Gospel! That is a really exciting mission as you partner with the Holy Spirit!

At the same time, we need to make a decision to bury those things once and for all... YES, those things that should never see the light of day! Don't be tempted by the enemy to dig them up!! Then the Holy Spirit will be able to perform another mystery of transformation in your life and there will be a coming forth in a new Resurrection Power reflecting the Majesty of God Himself!

"Dare to Receive the Treasures of Darkness and Hidden Riches of Secret Places!"

Chapter 18.

The Kingdom of Heaven is like: BURIED TREASURE... Precious PEARLS!

1 Corinthians 4:5 "He will bring to light the secret things that are hidden in the darkness". I love this Scripture because it confirms what the Holy Spirit says in Isaiah 45:3 "I will give you the treasures of darkness and hidden riches of secret places"! Throughout the whole Bible, these treasures and hidden riches are there for us to dig out and discover with the Holy Spirit's help!! That is SO exciting!!

Matthew 13:44, The Passion Translation, "Heaven's Kingdom realm can be illustrated like this: A man discovered that there was hidden treasure in a field. Upon finding it, he hid it again. Because of uncovering such treasure, he was overjoyed and sold all that he possessed to buy the entire field just so he could have the treasure".

The Spiritual Renewal Bible says: "The Kingdom of Heaven is like a treasure that a man discovered hidden in a field. In his excitement, he hid it again and sold everything he owned to get enough money to buy the field... and get the treasure too!"

There are several ways to look at this parable, but I will share how it speaks to me and trust that the Holy Spirit will highlight something special to encourage you!

Jesus represents the man who sold all He owned... Jesus left His exalted place in Glory with the Father to come and pay for the sin of the whole world with His own blood, just so He could have you and me as His treasure. Heaven's Kingdom realm is personally experienced when we realize what a great price Jesus paid for you and me... the cost was priceless... His own sacred life willingly laid down, and all His precious blood spilled out to redeem us! The re-hiding of the treasure is a hint of our new life hidden in God.

Yes! Feast on all the treasures of the Heavenly Realm!

Colossians 3:1-4 says in the Passion Translation... "Christ's resurrection is your resurrection too. This is why we are now to yearn and long for all that is above, for that's where Christ sits enthroned at the place of all power, honour and authority!

Fill your thoughts with heavenly realities, and not with the distractions of the natural realm. Your crucifixion with Christ has severed the tie to this life and now your true life is hidden away with God in Christ. And as Christ Himself is seen for who He really is THEN the miracle of who you really are will also be revealed because you are now one with Him in His glory"!

This really is the incredible Good News of the Gospel, and it would appear that Jesus so wanted to reveal these hidden treasures to His followers even though He knew that not everyone would understand, and He said, "I will utter things that have been hidden since the foundation of the world".

But now they are revealed to us by the Spirit... Hallelujah!

This parable would seem to be God's eternal perspective of how He viewed the extreme darkness of the world He had created and yet now this earth and this field appear as an uncultivated piece of land with little value! **BUT GOD sees differently** and as the Lord God Almighty sees with His perfect perception, He finds that there is buried treasure hidden in the field! Oh, the joy; Oh, the excitement; Oh, the thrill; Oh, the anticipation! The cost doesn't matter now because He knows that there is treasure hidden there!

So, God has to find a way to secure the field so that those treasures will not be lost but can be rescued for all eternity! Almighty God was prepared to give anything and everything to redeem His priceless treasures. But there was only one way... the only complete way that He could get His treasure back was to buy the whole field by giving His Only Begotten Son Jesus Christ to pay the price with His own life sacrificially laid down because there no one else could pay the debt!!

John 3:16, The Bible, says, "God so loved the world that He gave His only begotten Son, so that whoever believes in Him shall not perish but have eternal life". This demonstrates how much Father loves the world!

Oh Beloved, as you read this... I trust something of your own true intrinsic value and how precious and treasured you really are to God will begin to burn in your heart with such tremendous fire, passion and thanksgiving!? God sees you as His treasure and YES! We were hidden away in the darkness... but God the Father and the Holy Spirit saw us hidden and buried in the blackness of the world and He had to have you and me! So, Jesus became our wonderful Saviour who gave everything, even His own life, to buy us back from Satan's grasp!! All of the Triune God-Head was involved in making sure we became His Treasures!

WOW! This blows my mind! But it also thrills me to the core of my being!

Matthew 13:45-46 **A PRECIOUS PEARL**

Here is another parable demonstrating this Truth but in a different way!

"Again the Kingdom of Heaven is like a man who is a dealer in search of fine precious pearls who on finding a single pearl of great price, went and sold all he had and bought it."

The Passion Translation: "Heaven's Kingdom realm is also like a jewel merchant in search of rare pearls. When he discovered one precious and exquisite pearl, he immediately gave up all he had in exchange for it."

In this parable, Jesus is using the illustration of exquisite pearls (representing you and me) as an illustration of outstanding value and it really does show us how our Heavenly Lover goes looking for us His beloved ones! ... This is demonstrating God's extravagant love for us, His precious pearls,... and once again we see that no price was too high to pay! God literally killed Himself on the Cross to rescue you and me. There was no other way!

There had to be an exchange... In the Living Bible it says, 2 Corinthians 5:21 "For God took the sinless Christ and poured into Him our sins and then in exchange, He poured God's goodness into us!" So, the amazing value placed on each one of us is exactly same!! It was Jesus Christ's death that paid the price that determines the value... and it was the same for every single one of us!! Isn't that just so revealing? If you have a very low opinion of yourself as of being only of a little value, that is totally and completely wrong... especially if you happen to think someone else is of more value than you!!! Don't believe the lie of Satan!

So, for us a BIG mind-set adjustment is needed...

1 John 3:1 "See what an incredible love the Father has lavished on us that we should be called children of God... and that is what we are"! Each one of us is absolutely unique, God doesn't make duplicates... even identical twins have differences! So too with each precious pearl, it is totally unique, it is rare and SO beautiful.

It is interesting and very revealing how these pearls are formed within the soft living tissue of an Oyster. Each oyster is so soft and vulnerable on the inside that the only way it is kept safe is because it has the sanctuary of its hard shell to protect it! The oysters can only live because their shell that has two valves that open and shut to breathe the water in and out again. When this happens sometimes a minute grain of sand enters and attaches itself to the soft tissue inside the oyster. This causes great pain to the oyster... but amazingly it does not react negatively to try and get rid of the cause of the pain which is the grain of sand!

Instead it responds by releasing and wrapping the grain of sand in over-lapping thin layers of translucent solution called "mother of pearl." The more suffering the oyster experiences the more the "mother of pearl" solution is stimulated to pour out extra of the luminous liquid around the grain of sand, so forming a beautiful pearl little by little deep inside the heart of the oyster. This semi-transparent solution glows when it is seen from different angles and has a reflective beauty as light penetrates through the layers of "mother of pearl" as if it is alive!

As a small child, I loved my Nan, and I was fascinated with her beautiful string of pearls that she always wore. I remember her telling me why she hardly ever took them off... she explained that because they were real precious pearls, not imitation ones, they needed to be close to her skin, so they never lost their lustre. Perhaps you have noticed that our wonderful Queen also wears her pearls most of the time! No doubt they are real precious pearls that she treasures!!

During this time of incubation where the pearl is being formed in the soft tissue... the oyster clings steadfastly to a large secure rock deep on the ocean bed so that it is not washed away by the movement of the sea. So too for us, as we hold within us the **"Treasures of Darkness"** we need to cling to the Rock Christ Jesus!! He is the Rock of our Salvation and a hiding place from all the dangers around us!!

113

It is interesting that each pearl can only be harvested by the death of the oyster!

It is exactly the same for us as God's beautiful pearl treasures... we have been bought and redeemed by the death and blood of Jesus, God's Son. What happens is that the skilful divers are especially trained from a very young age to be able to hold their breath as they dive into the unfathomable depths of the ocean hunting for the oysters that contain the precious pearls. When they find one clinging to a rock, they use their knives to cut the oyster open and it is left for dead on the sea floor. However, the pearl is carefully rescued from inside the oyster and becomes the priceless treasure it is!

This is a very real lesson for us.... How do we respond to suffering?

It is possible for The Holy Spirit to make beautiful pearls out of the darkness of things that happen to us! Even the pain that can come from the traumas of life... like betrayal, unfair situations, disappointment, loss, sickness or rejection and a million other things that may have happened to you... ALL of them can become beautiful pearls... **"Treasures of Darkness"**. It all depends on how we respond?? **IF** we choose to allow the tender healing comfort of the Holy Spirit to bring the "Balm of Gilead" to wrap itself around us in those painful times, then I promise you that He will transform whatever suffering is being experienced into His special treasures. Yes! Just like the pearl in the oyster!

The Kingdom of Heaven is made up of precious pearls that Jesus has rescued from the very depths of despair and He wants to put His pearls on display to show forth His Glory!! In Malachi 3:17 The Bible says, "They shall be Mine says the Lord of Hosts, in that day when I publicly and openly declare them to be MY Jewels, My Special Possession and My Peculiar Treasure".

So, my dear precious child of God, whoever you are, please believe that the Lord of Glory has gone to the utter most lengths of extreme darkness to redeem you... no one is more precious than you are! You have been harvested to be for His Glory and to demonstrate that you really are **"His Treasure of Darkness"**. When we bow at His feet and worship Him around the Throne, we will have an opportunity to express our love and adoration to Him for all eternity as the Treasures he has won!! In the meantime, we have a choice whether we really do desire to make an entire offering of our whole lives to serve Him, honour Him and follow Him with complete devotion as an expression of our love for Jesus!

"Dare to Receive the Treasures of Darkness"

Chapter 19.

Treasures in Two Storms

Mark 4:35-41 Passion Translation... **THE FIRST STORM**

"Later that day, after it grew very dark, Jesus said to His disciples, "Let us cross over to the other side of the lake". After they had sent the crowd away, they shoved off from shore with Him, as he had been teaching from the boat, and there were other boats that sailed with them. Suddenly, as they were crossing the lake, a ferocious tempest arose, with violent winds and waves that were crashing into the boat until it was all but swamped. But Jesus was calmly sleeping in the stern, resting on a cushion. So, they shook Him awake, saying, "Teacher, don't you even care that we are all about to die"! Fully awake, He rebuked the storm and shouted to the sea, "Hush! Calm down!" All at once the wind stopped howling and the water became perfectly calm. Then He turned to His disciples and said to them, "Why are you so afraid? Haven't you learned to trust yet?" But they were overwhelmed with fear and awe and said to one another, "Who is this man who has such authority that even the wind and the waves obey Him?"

As we have been treasure hunting through the Bible with the Holy Spirit, we have seen constantly that the enemy works in the darkness! Here, in the storm... we see that **after it grew very dark...** Satan is again trying to kill Jesus and his disciples! In some other versions of the Bible, it tells us that the storm was of hurricane proportions and it came up from below very suddenly!

I remember a few years ago that I was on the beach here in Mallorca relaxing and enjoying myself... when suddenly I noticed some people were packing up and leaving in a hurry! While others were huddled under the beach brollies for shelter and I wondered what was going on... then I noticed huge big ominous black clouds gathering very quickly and the wind had suddenly got up and I soon felt huge drops of rain!! A storm had arrived very unexpectedly... I was just wondering what to do when the Holy Spirit whispered to me! "Gill there is a way to enjoy a storm... just watch!" As I watched with a new interest, I noticed a group of people had left the beach and gone down into the water, they were thoroughly enjoying being in the waves even as the rain started to pour down!

Quietly the Holy Spirit said, "Gill you can run from the darkness of a storm and it will follow you or you can try to shelter in fear and the darkness will trap you. But the best way is to decide to trust that the storm will pass, find the eye of the storm and enjoy My Presence being assured that I will protect you". WOW! That was such a different way to look at the darkness of a storm!

Sometimes God calms the storm and sometimes He lets the storm rage and calms His child!!

So, what happened here in the Bible? For the disciples in this particular storm… they had not been disobedient, but they demonstrated that they were keen to be obedient and to follow Jesus, and they had obeyed His word to get into the boat. They had His promise to go to the other side of the lake and more than anything Jesus was actually there with them in the boat! All the right things to do!! Most of them were obviously experienced fishermen so they would have recognised any adverse weather signs… BUT darkness can produce sudden storms in our lives as well as on the lake!! For Jesus… He is resting, He is asleep in the stern of the boat… He is in Father's arms. He is Prince of Peace!

We need to learn how to sleep in a storm!

For the disciples they can't run away… there is nowhere for them to go, and fear does strange things in the darkness. So, they do the right thing to call on Jesus BUT not in the right spirit… it was not right to blame Him!! "Master, don't you care that we are perishing?" At every instance in our lives we need to remember that Jesus' prime mission is in training His disciples to do the right thing in the face of any darkness or any storm that we might be experiencing. At this precise time Jesus didn't answer their wrong assumption that He didn't care… **of course He did care! He always cares!!** No! He simply arose and rebuked the wind and spoke to the waves… "Hush, calm down!" The blessing of the calm was experienced by all the other boats too… Hallelujah!

What I noticed particularly here is that there appeared to be two forces at work causing the ferocious storm… the wind and the waves… representing the enemy and the flesh! Jesus rebuked the wind and then He spoke to the waves! Whenever we encounter any sort of storm, we need to follow Jesus' example… **Rebuke the devil and Speak to our fleshly reactions.** It is the devil that stirs up the waves that affects our flesh! We need to discern what the enemy is doing, deal with that first, and then

117

speak directly to the circumstances. Fear paralyses and has two reactions... Run or Hide? Be careful not to do either!! Jesus taught His disciples in this particular instance by modelling in front of them how to deal with a storm! But He also directly addresses their fears and their lack of faith... "Why are you so timid and fearful? How is it you have no faith?"

Yes! Jesus did protect them in this extremely dark moment of danger, but they did not personally **"Receive the Treasures of Darkness"** that were there for them! The reason was that fear blinded them as to who Jesus really was! They addressed him as Teacher or as in some other versions: Master! We need to be sure we know who is in our boat!! Then also it was their unbelief that made them forget that they actually had the word of God... "Go to the other side!" We are told that, "The disciples were filled with great awe and feared exceedingly and said to one another..."

"Who is this, that the wind and sea obey him?"

For us, in any storm or darkness these are essential guidelines for us all!

1. We must have The Word of God...Jesus is our anchor and He is the Living Word of God and He alone will keep us secure.

2. We must guard against any fear taking hold of us and confront it immediately as 2 Timothy1:7 says: "God has not given us a spirit of fear but of love, power and a sound mind."

3. The Bible says in James 4:7 "Submit to God and resist the devil and he will flee from you."

4. Zechariah 4:6 "Not by might, nor by power, but by My Spirit," says the Lord.

THEN we are ready to "Receive the Treasures of Darkness."

Matthew 14: 22-33 Passion Translation......**THE SECOND STORM**

"As soon as the people were fed, Jesus told the disciples to get into their boat and go to the other side of the lake while he stayed behind

118

to dismiss the people. After the crowds dispersed, Jesus went up into the hills to pray.

And as night fell... Jesus was there praying alone to God. But the disciples, who were now in the middle of the lake, ran into trouble, for their boat was tossed by the high winds and heavy seas. At about four o'clock in the morning, Jesus came to them, walking on the waves! When the disciples saw him walking on top of the water, they were terrified and screamed, "A Ghost!" Then Jesus said, "Be brave and don't be afraid; I AM here!" Peter shouted out, "Lord, if it's really you, then have me join you on the water!"

"Come and join me" ... Jesus replied.

So, Peter stepped out onto the water and began to walk toward Jesus, but when he realized how high the waves were, he became frightened and started to sink. "Save me, Lord!" Peter cried out. Jesus immediately stretched out his hand and lifted him up and said, "What little faith you have! Why would you let doubt win?" And that very moment as they both climbed into the boat, the raging wind ceased. Then all the disciples crouched down before Him and worshipped Jesus.

They said in adoration, "You are truly the Son of God!"

As we look at this second storm incident some things are very similar and others very different... To begin with, Jesus had directed the disciples to get into the boat and go before him to the other side! They had the word! But this time they were on their own, Jesus stayed behind to deal with the 5000 crowd that had been fed with five loaves and two small fish!!

Again, it was night and the darkness had fallen. After the great miracle it's no wonder that the enemy stirs up a storm... we don't look for it, but we need to be alert to recognise his devious plans. The disciples were obedient on each occasion going towards the goal of the other side of the lake. We are told that by the time that the boat was almost a mile distant from land... suddenly their boat was being beaten and tossed by the waves, for the wind was against them! Obviously, they must have been rowing really hard for a long time and getting nowhere!!

It is worth recognising that our own efforts will never be sufficient to save us!

But what should encourage us, is that even though Jesus was not actually in the boat with them, he was fully aware of their difficulties as he was praying on the hillside overlooking the lake. Remember in Hebrews 2:17-18 that "Jesus has become our merciful and faithful High Priest... and he is able immediately to run to the cry of those who are being tested and tried and exposed to suffering". Isn't that marvellous?

So, at the very darkest hour in the fourth watch, between 3.00am and 6.00am Jesus arrives to help his disciples... but not as they might have expected! Remember that darkness always distorts and brings illusions. Emotions get stirred up and fear blinds us from seeing Jesus! But here Jesus comes to them walking on top of the waves. The disciples have never seen this before... it's outside their experience! Jesus demonstrates that He is always above the storms of life and never under the circumstances! However, the disciples don't recognise him and come to a wrong conclusion!! They think it's a Ghost!

Remember, whatever problems you or I might have... Jesus is on top of them! Darkness and Storms are not a problem to Him... they are opportunities for Him to give us special **"Treasures of Darkness"** that will increase our faith and deepen our knowledge of who Jesus really is! Again, as in the first storm, straight away Jesus speaks and confronts their fears, "Take courage! I AM! Stop being afraid!" But this time Jesus says who He is... I AM! This is the holy, sacred and revered name of the Lord God Himself!

I don't know if Peter may have recognised Jesus' voice or perhaps it was what He actually said: I AM... But, whatever, Peter takes a huge risk as he responds, "If it is you, command me to come to you on the water!" I have a big imagination and can just see Peter dumbfounded as Jesus voice booms out to him over the noise of the waves crashing against the boat... "COME!" Then, I can see Peter taking an enormous leap of faith into the roaring waves as he fixed his eyes steadfastly on Jesus and actually walked out on the Word of God!

We must never look down on Peter because he failed, but realize he is the only person in the Bible who ever walked on water with Jesus!! Yes! Peter did take his eyes off Jesus! Yes! He did look down! Yes! He did get overcome with fear as he felt the strong wind and began to sink... **BUT, Peter cried out,** "Lord, save me!" And we read that instantly Jesus reached out His hand and caught and held him!

I believe that Jesus was absolutely thrilled because Peter had taken that step of faith and responded to the invitation to "COME!" So likewise, I believe Jesus will be pleased when any of us take a risk to come to Jesus in our darkness or in any storm we might face. Jesus said, "O you of little faith, why did you doubt?" And together they walked on the water back to the boat and the wind ceased!!!

This was not a rebuke in my opinion, but Jesus was encouraging Peter by saying... "Look what you can do with just a little faith, now see what can be accomplished if you don't let doubt creep in!" We too are told in: Hebrews 12:2 "Fix our eyes on Jesus the Author, Finisher and the Source of our faith... He is our Leader and the One Who enables us!

SO where are "The Treasures of Darkness" in this storm?

This is where this storm really produced all the treasures Jesus planned for His disciples... The result: "All the disciples crouched down before Him and worshipped Jesus. **They said in adoration, "You truly are the Son of God!"** They all had a new revelation of Who Jesus really was... When this happens then we too can surely...

"Dare to Receive the Treasures of Darkness!"

CHAPTER 20.

Treasures of Transformation... for a WOMAN!

Sometimes I meet people who have been so deeply damaged in their lives, that they will often share their most horrific stories with me and my heart goes out to them as they can end up believing that their life is far too bad for the Lord to ever use them or even change them. It can seem that way... but there is always the power of testimony that reveals: **"Nothing is impossible to God!"** My own testimony always encourages people to believe that what God has done for me He can do for them... no-one is beyond hope or beyond His touch!!

They are still "His Treasures."

But I also know that however, poignant a testimony is, it is very important to be able to see the equivalent in the Word of God! So, I want to share with you that lasting transformation can really happen when you meet Jesus!

A Woman of Darkness meets Jesus!

John 8:1-12 "But Jesus went to the Mount of Olives early in the morning, He came back into the temple court, and the people came to Him in crowds. He sat down and was teaching them, when the Scribes and Pharisees brought in a woman who had been caught in adultery. They made her stand in the middle of the court and put the case before Him. "Teacher" they said, "this woman has been caught in the very act of adultery, now Moses in the Law commanded us that such women shall be stoned to death. **But what do you say to do with her... what is your sentence?"** This they said to try and test Him, hoping they might find a charge to accuse Him. But Jesus stooped down and wrote on the ground with His finger.

However, when they persisted with their questions, He raised Himself up and said, "Let him who is without sin among you be the first to throw a stone at her". Then He bent down again and went on writing on the ground with His finger, they listened to Him, and then they began going out conscience stricken, one by one, from the oldest down to the last one of them; till Jesus was left alone with the woman standing there before

Him in the centre of the court. When Jesus raised Himself up, He said to her, **"Woman where are your accusers? Has no man condemned you?"** She answered, "No-one, Lord!" And Jesus said, "I do not condemn you either. Go your way and from now on sin no more". Once more Jesus addressed the crowd and said," I am the Light of the world and he who follows Me will not be walking in the dark but will have the Light which is Life".

This clearly shows the limitless mercy of God displayed in Jesus Christ.

But it also shows us that the Scribes and Pharisees are out to get Jesus... using a woman in deep dark trouble and captive to the powers of darkness. What I love about this is that Jesus doesn't see her darkness, **He sees her potential** and He made a point to come back down from His prayer time on the Mount of Olives for this one woman, and He still does that today!! Jesus sees our need beforehand and is always there to help us!

He was sitting in the place of authority and teaching the crowds, Jesus is in the public place of the temple courtyard when His accusers bring in this woman caught in the act of adultery. They should have brought in the man as well, but they didn't... so the Scribes and Pharisees were bending the Law to suit themselves to trap Jesus. She would probably have been naked and more or less dragged in by her hair and made to stand in the centre of the court... vulnerable and her guilt exposed for all to see! This dear woman was in a hopeless situation, full of shame and fear as she knew she faced death by stoning. I can only imagine how her head hung down and her heart beating fast as she listened to the way they were asking Jesus for His sentence on her. I know that the crowd must have been silent, staring at Jesus and waiting in anticipation as to hear what He would say...

We are told Jesus stooped down and wrote on the ground with His finger, even as the Scribes and Pharisees kept on pushing Jesus for an answer, so He raised Himself up and spoke... as the Passion Translation says, **"Let's have the man who has never had a sinful desire throw the first stone at her"**. Then He bent over again and wrote some more words in the dust!

I can only guess what it must have been like... the awesome atmosphere and anointing of the Presence of God filling that courtyard as Jesus spoke those words. We are not told what Jesus was writing, but it was the same "finger of God" who wrote the 10 Commandments on the tablet on Mount Sinai, and also the prophecy written on the wall that terrified the king in the book of Daniel.

The Holy Spirit is recognised as the "finger of God" and it must have been a really awesome moment! We know that Jesus continued speaking because it says, "they were listening, even as He continued to write in the dust". There must have been such a deep conviction of sin among them that all the accusers just couldn't stay in the Presence of such holiness... So they went out one by one... the oldest first! WOW!

Now Jesus found Himself left alone with this woman, who was standing there before Him. He raised Himself up again and spoke to her, "Woman where are your accusers? Has no man condemned you?" Imagine such a powerful anointing and the woman with her head hung down, but now she looks up for the first time, hears His voice and sees no-one is left. Then, I believe she would have looked and seen the eyes of Jesus Christ Himself with such love and compassion embracing her!!

"This was a beautiful treasure of transformation!"

Just her and Jesus! And when she says: "No-one, Lord!" She is saying in Aramaic: "MarYah" ... in other words, **You are my Lord Yahweh!!** This woman in her moment of destiny has a Divine Revelation of who Jesus really is! In His response, Jesus says, "I don't condemn you either, but go and from now on, be free from your life of sin". Then He declares "I am the Light of the world and anyone who follows me will not be walking in the dark but will have the Light which is Life".

I am sure that as this woman heard those last words of Jesus she knew she would never be walking in darkness again... her life has been totally transformed! I just love to see the mercy and loving compassion of Jesus and personally I know just a little of how she must have felt that day! She expected death and received life, she was unclean and now she had been made clean! This woman had become a completely transformed redeemed child of God.

"What a Real Treasure of Darkness!"

But somehow I knew there was more to this encounter than I was seeing! As I prayed in the Spirit, it was then that the Holy Spirit opened up the Word to me in a new way and I want to link up another Scripture with this one because, I believe, this was only the beginning of the full story of this woman. Be open to see this in a new light and live this experience with the Holy Spirit!

What would this woman do after her dramatic Life-Changing Encounter?

All I know is that after I personally met with the Lord Jesus Christ Himself I wanted to give Him everything....I was SO thankful for His mercy! I wanted desperately to express just how grateful I was for the blood that cleansed me and I was over-whelmed by His forgiveness and His amazing love that had saved me from hell!!

So, as I was pondering this, the Holy Spirit whispered to me "Luke 7:37-50". At the time I was not aware what was written in this particular Scripture. Then as I read it, the Lord's small still voice said, "This is the same Mary... Mary Magdalene... from whom seven demons were expelled."

Suddenly I understand what had happened! Of course, ... she would have gone back to her room... probably going over and over in her mind what had just taken place! I am sure it was a mixture of wonder and excitement bubbling up with the incredible events of what had happened to her! Maybe it was her own room where she had had to hide her terrible shame and secrets of her life of prostitution from the rest of the family? I can just imagine her looking around what could she give Jesus? How could she say thank you? How could she express all she felt? How could she reveal her throbbing heart of joy and thankfulness?

Then as she looked, I can visualize that all of a sudden... she saw the alabaster jar filled with pure Nard, which is the most expensive perfume. Oh! Was it possible that Jesus would accept such a gift from someone like her? Excitement, yes, but trembling too, as she planned to give it all to Jesus! Personally, I began to research how Mary could have had such an expensive alabaster jar of pure nard since she was a harlot?

There must be an answer!!

I found out that in those days, the rich men from the east would stop off at Bethany just outside Jerusalem. These men were looking for satisfaction with a prostitute before going on into the city after their long journey. They usually had a small flask on their body with this pure nard in it and depending on the pleasure they received they would put; one, two or three drops in the prostitutes' jar as payment. With the body warmth the Spikenard softened it like liquid but as soon as it was put in an alabaster translucent marble jar it would solidify. The perfume came from the root and spike of the Nard plant found in Northern India and was the most costly perfume. For these rich men it was their means of money!

Now I saw it, Hallelujah!!...

Mary must have seen the alabaster jar filled with the Spikenard perfume. It was the only valuable thing she possessed, and it represented all her dark shame-filled life of immorality and it must have seemed like a stench of her unclean past... YET... here was this most costly perfume! It was her only insurance for the future, and it was all she had of value at this present time! In that moment Mary decided, there in her room, she just had to go and anoint Jesus... She would pour out all the perfume on the only One who was worthy! She wanted to give her best treasure to Jesus! I can imagine her tears of joy as she made up her mind that this was the only way she could express her over-flowing heart to say a real thank you to Him!!

BUT where was this Jesus who had saved her life?

As Mary asked around, she heard He was at Simon, the leper's house! Now she had decided! It had got to be NOW! Nothing was going to stop her!!! Let's read the account in the Bible...

Luke 7: 37-50 "One of the Pharisees asked Jesus to dine with him and Jesus went into Simon's house and reclined at table. Behold, a woman of the town who was an especially wicked sinner, when she learned that He was reclining at table in the Pharisee's house, she bought an alabaster flask of expensive perfume. Standing behind Jesus at His feet weeping, she began to wet His feet with her tears; and she wiped them with the hair of her head and kissed His feet and anointed them with the perfume. Now when Simon who had invited Jesus saw it, he said to himself... if this man were a prophet, He would surely know who and what sort of woman this is who is touching Him... for she is a notorious sinner devoted to sin."

And Jesus, replying, said to him "Simon, I have something to say to you". And he answered, "Teacher, say it." A certain lender of money had two debtors; one owed him five hundred Denarii and the other fifty. When they had no means of paying, he freely forgave them both. Now which of them will love him more? Simon answered, "The one for whom he forgave

126

and cancelled more". And Jesus said to him, "you have decided correctly".

Then turning toward the woman, He said to Simon, "Do you see this woman? When I came into your house, you gave me no water to wash my feet, but she has wet my feet with her tears and wiped them with her hair. You gave me no kiss, but she from the moment I came in has not ceased to kiss my feet tenderly. You did not anoint my head with ordinary oil, but she has anointed my feet with costly rare perfume. Therefore, I tell you, her sins, many as they are, are forgiven her... because she has loved much. But he who is forgiven little loves little".

And Jesus said to her, "Your sins are forgiven!"

Then those who were at table with Him began to say among themselves. "Who is this who even forgives sins?" But Jesus said to the woman... "Your faith has saved you; go in peace, in freedom from all the distresses that are experienced as the result of sin."

Many things have struck me from this portion of God's Word... one was that Simon, the leper must have been healed at some time by Jesus or he could not have invited Him to his house, otherwise he would have been in the valley of the lepers outside the town! So, inviting Jesus into his house for a meal was his way of showing gratitude! BUT his heart was still full of self-righteousness judgement and pride which Jesus was so clever to confront asking Simon to make a judgement on himself!

So, for Simon there was NO TREASURE to give to Jesus!

We too, must be so careful, and we also need to realize that Jesus reads our thoughts and attitudes and not just what we say!! When Jesus finally exposed what Simon had NOT done for Him, He praised Mary for what she HAD done in total contrast! We need to be reminded that there are sins of omission as well as sins we actually do! Both need to be repented of!! We do not see in this passage any fruit that Simon was showing, even though he must have met with Jesus prior to this particular evening! Again, this should really warn us that every encounter which Jesus so graciously allows us to have with Him... whether in receiving healings or answers to prayers or even just bringing us His comfort... there must be evidence in our everyday lives and our attitudes to others, that Jesus has changed us. It is by our fruit we shall be known!

We need to check ourselves and keep short accounts!!

Mary, on the other hand, making her way to Simon's house, would have had to put her really bad reputation of her past out of her mind and instead focus on getting to Jesus and giving Him her everything... After all, she was a completely new person now since she had met Jesus! As she would have done that, I am sure that new supernatural courage and boldness would have surged up from deep inside her spirit as she actually gate-crashed the party! Nothing was going to stop her getting to Jesus!

Many of the disciples, including Judas, tried to stop her. They just couldn't understand why this well-known harlot woman of such ill-repute was there at all and certainly not bringing this expensive perfume... they thought it would have been better to sell it and bless the poor.

BUT Mary was on a mission... she was absolutely determined to press on to her goal of getting to the feet of Jesus... she had eyes for no one else!! When you have truly personally encountered the Lord Jesus Christ Himself, He is the One you love more than anybody and anything else! Jesus responds to this sort of devotion! He immediately defends Mary and in one of the other Gospel accounts, Jesus said, "She has done a beautiful thing for me"! Isn't that fantastic?

Jesus could have looked at her offering of ill-gotten gains and refused them; but He saw her heart and it didn't bother Him that she was caressing His body as she anointed Him with the rare perfume. Jesus saw **"Treasures of Darkness"** and her tears blessed Him as He accepted her radical expression of total passionate love. In another passage we are told that Mary smashed the alabaster jar so that she could get all of the solidified perfume out more quickly to fully anoint her Lord!

Such was her burning love!

I wonder if you know what it really meant when Mary wiped His feet with her hair?

In those days the only time a young woman, in the presence of a man, was allowed to untie her hair and let it hang loose would have been on her bridal night! Here, we see Mary as she unties her hair and uses it to wipe Jesus' feet as her tears splashed down on His feet. This revealed reason is so special because it is a demonstration of absolute surrender... it is her symbol of saying, "I am your beloved and I am wedded to you forever".

Isn't that just SO wonderful? Every gesture that Mary made demonstrated that she was now totally sold out and transformed and then Jesus even says to her, "Your faith has saved you".

John 12:3 **"And the whole house was filled with the fragrance of the perfume!"**

One of the most marvellous things to me it that Jesus completely received and accepted Mary... but He also received her gift! There is nothing that we could ever do to earn our Salvation... Jesus saves us out His love and mercy and that is:

PURE UNDESERVED GRACE!!

Later on we see Mary is always there with Jesus, she is one of the women who ministers to His needs and she is there at His feet listening to His teaching and she was there at the Cross... she is there near by the Tomb and she is there in the Garden and she meets her Risen Christ! She was the first evangelist to be commissioned by Jesus to: **"Go and tell..."**

Such beautiful fruit that glorifies the Lord Jesus! That is our certainty too that... what Jesus could do for her, He is able and willing to do for anyone who comes to Him in humility and has a heart that is open and filled with thanksgiving and has a fire and passion with love for Him... no matter how dreadful our past has been... He is the Merciful Redeemer!!

Mary has become a "Transformed Treasure of Darkness" and brings Light Wherever she goes... Hallelujah!!

Chapter 21.

Treasures revealed in Darkness for SAUL!

As I researched the subject of a terrorist, I came across this definition: "A terrorist is a person who premeditates violence to create a climate of fear and intimidation as a means of coercion in pursuit of a political or religious aim involving dangers to human life". You must be wondering why this chapter is called "Treasures revealed in Darkness? I think you will understand as you read on!!!

Saul, who later became Paul, the Apostle, perfectly fits this description...
I think you will agree!?

Acts 9:1-22 "Saul still drawing his breath hard from threatening and murderous desire against the disciples of the Lord went to the high priest and requested of him letters to the synagogues at Damascus authorizing him so that if he found any men or women belonging to the Way of life determined by faith in Jesus Christ, he might bring them bound with chains to Jerusalem".

Now as he travelled on, he came near Damascus, and suddenly a light from heaven flashed around him, and he fell to the ground. Then he heard a voice saying to him, "Saul, Saul, why are you persecuting, harassing, troubling and molesting me?" And Saul said, "Who are you Lord?" And He said, "I am Jesus, whom you are persecuting. It is dangerous and it will turn out badly for you to keep kicking against the goad to offer vain and perilous resistance". Trembling and astonished he asked, "Lord, what do you want me to do?" The Lord said to him, "Arise and go into the city, and you will be told what you must do".

The men who were accompanying him were unable to speak for terror, hearing the voice but seeing no one. Then Saul got up from the ground, but though his eyes were opened, he could see nothing; so, they led him by the hand and brought him into Damascus. And he was unable to see for three days, and he neither ate nor drank anything.

Now there was in Damascus a disciple named Ananias. The Lord said to him in a vision, "Ananias," And he answered, "Here I am Lord".

And the Lord said to him, "Get up and go to the street called Straight and ask at the house of Judas for a man of Tarsus named Saul, for behold, he is praying there and has seen in a vision a man named Ananias enter and lay his hands on him so that he might regain his sight".

But Ananias answered, "Lord, I have heard many people tell about this man, especially how much evil and what great suffering he has brought on your saints at Jerusalem; now he is here and has authority from the high priests to put in chains all who call upon your Name". But the Lord said to him, "Go, for this man is a chosen instrument of mine to bear my Name before Gentiles and kings and the descendants of Israel; for I will make clear to him how much he will be afflicted and must suffer for my Name's sake".

So, Ananias left and went into the house. And he laid hands on Saul and said, "Brother Saul, the Lord Jesus, who appeared to you along the way by which you came here, has sent me that you may recover your sight and be filled with the Holy Spirit". And instantly something like scales fell from Saul's eyes, and he recovered his sight. Then he arose and was baptized and after he took some food, he was strengthened. For several days afterward he remained with the disciples at Damascus. And immediately in the synagogue he proclaimed Jesus, saying, "He is the Son of God!" And all who heard him were amazed and said, "Is this not the very man who harassed and overthrew and destroyed in Jerusalem those who called upon this Name? And he was come here for the express purpose of arresting them and bringing them in chains before the chief priests". But Saul increased all the more in strength, and continued to confound and put to confusion the Jews who lived in Damascus by comparing and examining evidence and proving that Jesus is the Christ Messiah!

Saul was a real terrorist if ever there was one... he had set out to intimidate and to imprison and do harm to Jesus' followers there in Damascus just as he had done in Jerusalem. You could say he was a dangerous religious killer on the war path!! He was an aristocrat, highly intelligent, an expert in the religious Law of the Pharisees and a man of influence who was full of hatred that Satan had stirred up against the new believers. He was blinkered, and religion always wants to suppress and kill the real Truth! Saul was not the sort of person we would have chosen to demonstrate **"Treasures of Darkness"**! But in Isaiah 55:8 the Bible says, "My thoughts are not your thoughts, neither are your ways my ways, says the Lord".

I would like to share a real true story with you!

At the time Skippy and I were pastors of our first church in Buxton in Derbyshire in the 1980's, we were asked to host a visiting speaker for our mid-week meeting; he was on furlough and visiting many AOG Churches to up-date those who supported his ministry in the Far East. Adam came to our house for a meal beforehand and seemed very quiet and was very small in stature, a young man with not a lot to say... except he asked to see what spices I had in my kitchen cupboard as he was used to very spicy food! Skippy and I wondered how he was going to share with our congregation that evening as he seemed so shy and reluctant to engage in conversation.

We need not have been concerned, the moment Adam stepped onto the platform the anointing came on him and this was what he shared... to begin with he pulled down his lower lip and showed everyone his terrorist IRA number!! He had been an active IRA terrorist in Northern Ireland!! He was known as apparently a particularly notorious killer who was not averse to killing people on sight! As you can guess, our congregation was riveted to hear more!

This was Adam's story that he shared with us that night as I remember it...

Apparently, it was on one particular windy evening when he set out to kill any protestant civilians that happened to be around... BUT that night the streets seemed strangely deserted! So, he moved along in the shadows with his gun at the ready, loaded to kill whoever moved!! Suddenly he heard a door creak open and he was all ready to fire... when he saw a small figure there in the doorway and recognised that it was an elderly Nun in her habit. Normally he would have shot first, but he didn't that night! Startled he heard her begin to speak to him and she called him by name... she said, "Adam the Lord Jesus has just appeared to me in my room while I was praying and He told me to come out here in the street and to tell you that Jesus loves you and died for you and He has a plan for your life"! Then she disappeared inside the Convent and he heard the door slam behind her!

That simple word from a little old Nun on a blustery windy night in the back streets of Belfast was what changed his life!! Adam met with the love of Jesus and he told us how he had been completely transformed, how he had repented and received the forgiveness of Jesus at the Cross and was washed clean by the shed blood of Christ and became a New Creation! He went on to tell us his story and how the Lord had miraculously qualified him as a Missionary and how he had been sent to the remote areas of Borneo where he had planted over a thousand churches!!! That night there wasn't a dry eye in the Church and several people re-dedicated their whole lives to serving the Lord Jesus!

Adam had been a real live terrorist who God got hold of and Adam realized the storehouse of "The Treasures of Darkness" that the Lord had planted in him and now he was spending his life giving them all away to glorify his beloved Jesus who had saved him.

I hope that has inspired you!!

Back to Saul... The really sad thing I feel about Saul at this time was that he really believed he was doing the right thing. Like so many of us... we too can be blinded by the lies of Satan. Oh Lord, please open our eyes to see the Truth that will set us free! Because if Saul could be so completely WRONG and was utterly deceived by the enemy... so it is possible it could happen to us! Saul had already committed murder in condoning the execution of Stephen, the first Christian martyr who was stoned to death. We read in Acts 8:3 "Saul shamefully treated and laid waste the church continuously with cruelty and violence entering house after house he dragged out men and women and committed them to prison". Saul had all the right papers and documents from the officials for his evil deeds and he was **ALMOST** there in Damascus to do his murderous plan!
BUT GOD stopped him and put a stop to Satan's plans!

Perhaps, this is a moment to really thank the Lord for every time He has prevented some terrible things happening in your life! Some things we may be aware of, others we do not know... but I am sure that angels have protected us all on numerous occasions and even healed relationships when everything seemed to be falling apart! How faithful is our God in every way!! I am SO thankful to you my God and my King! One personal memory is how the Lord intervened on three occasions as I set out to end my life but because I loved my children SO much... I turned around and changed my mind ... Oh Thank You Jesus! Let the Holy Spirit remind you how He has stepped in and stopped Satan's plans over your life and allow thankfulness to well up from deep within you!?

It is true you can run from God, but you cannot hide from Him!

Psalm 139:12 "Even the darkness is light to Him!" I am sure that the saints in Jerusalem and even in Damascus and the surrounding areas were all earnestly praying against what Saul was doing! But I am sure that they never even dreamed of the revelation of just how the Lord was going to answer their prayers!!! Saul came very close to carrying out his destructive terrorist mission!

That was when Saul was confronted with the REAL LIGHT exploding around him from Heaven. One version says, it was a light brighter than the mid-day sun! You could say that Jesus Christ allowed the darkness to envelope this murderous terrorist and Saul was completely blinded! His whole life was in the darkness now! There was such an intensity of this light that Saul literally fell to the ground.

Much later it was the same Saul, who had become the Apostle Paul, who wrote to Timothy about this supernatural light that blinded him!! 1 Timothy 6:15-16 says, "The King of kings and Lord of lords, who alone has immortality and lives in unapproachable light Who no man has ever seen or can see. Unto Him we give the honour and everlasting power and dominion".

Don't you think it is so incredible that The Lord asks Saul a question... "Why are you persecuting me? The Lord addresses him personally and then explains that all his aggression and hatred is really against the Lord Jesus Christ Himself and not the followers of "The Way!" That must have been a real revelation! This tells me that how we treat each other is really against Jesus ,or conversely it will reveal our love for Him as we extend His love to others! Oh, Holy Spirit help us to love one another the way Jesus loved us!

It was in the darkness that Saul met Jesus as Lord of all....

However, Saul doesn't recognise Him and has to ask, "Who are you Lord?" Then the Lord reveals Himself as "The Victorious One!" Saul is having a conversation with God and wants to immediately DO something for the Lord! That can be our attitude to want to "DO" something, when The Holy Spirit wants to direct our lives on the new pathway He has for us! Old ways have to change! Saul is told to get up and go into the city where he will be told what he is to do! The men with him are listening to everything being said... but they are stunned and speechless because they cannot see anyone! The whole situation is bizarre!! It is Heaven invading earth to bring into the light **"The Treasures of Darkness"** hidden inside this infamous terrorist that neither Saul himself, nor anyone else knew were there!

Can you imagine Saul getting up and stumbling about, then suddenly realizing he cannot see at all and he is blind and groping about! How can he go anywhere when he can't see anything? The darkness is covering his whole being! Once he was in charge, leading the men on a terrorist mission... NOW Saul needs the men to lead him into the city! How humbling is that??? He used to have eyesight and could see clearly, and he used to be in charge, but now God wants Saul to have INSIGHT to see the treasure and potential that God sees in him. Now God is in charge! It's like Saul actually stumbled into experiencing and sharing the death and resurrection of Jesus Christ over those three days and nights while he fasted and had no drink. Oh, how the Holy Spirit was turning everything around... our walk has to be a walk of faith... not by sight!!

Saul was catapulted into this new walk of utter dependency on the Holy Spirit!!

Eyesight sees circumstances! **BUT INSIGHT sees TRUTH and HOPE** and enables us to see from God's Spiritual perspective. For the Lord to produce His hidden treasures, maybe we all need the darkness at some point in our lives; so that we can be enveloped with the glorious Light of the Gospel which is the power unto Salvation. Real Light needs to really pierce our hearts and cause a radical transformation in our innermost being! When the Lord allows the darkness in our lives, He always has a very special purpose and is working deep within us developing the treasures hidden away so we can accomplish His purposes and fulfil our destiny!

Darkness is not the end... but can be the beginning of something beautiful!

The Holy Spirit will be incubating something of eternal value deep inside us, just like a photo in negative form has to be taken into the dark room to be developed... so God is bringing forth very special **"Treasures of Darkness"**! When the Lord is dealing with us, we must be very careful not to be impatient and spoil what God is doing just because we might find waiting hard!

2 Corinthians 4:6-7 For God who said, "Let light shine out of darkness, has shone in our hearts so as to beam forth the light for the illumination of the knowledge of the majesty and glory of God as it is manifest in the Person and is revealed in the face of Jesus Christ. However, we possess this precious treasure in frail human vessels of earth that the

grandeur and exceeding greatness of the power may be shown to be from God and not from ourselves".

Unlimited treasures await us in those dark times and hidden riches of the secret places! Praise God! Before we ever see the treasure... God has prepared it and sees it and is just waiting to bring those treasures into the light! I believe Saul learnt to personally feast on Jesus as his Bread of Life during those three days of darkness; we are not told the mysteries that were encountered!

"Hidden Riches of Secret Places" ... but we all see the fruit!!

Even Saul needed someone to help him and perhaps it was really imperative for such a self-made man like Saul to again be humbled and ministered to by another man... so the Lord commissioned a believer called Ananias! How I can relate to this faithful man, how difficult he must have found it when the Holy Spirit gave him his instructions!! So, he did what I guess many of us tend to do... he told The Lord everything that the Lord already knew about why he shouldn't be obedient!

As I read again about Ananias I realized once more, just how important is our daily time with the Lord... What if Ananias had been too busy that morning? He would have missed the opportunity to partner with the Holy Spirit, missed the vision, missed being in the Bible! He would have missed seeing the miracle of a blind man's eyes open... Oh, I am sure that the Lord would have found someone else, but for Ananias, he would have lost out! Remember it is true that the Holy Spirit is not looking for our expertise but for our availability and willingness even when we feel inadequate!

So come on dearest fellow Believer, make sure you are faithful to your fellowship time with the Holy Spirit every day and expect an encounter, expect a revelation, expect The Lord to speak... He is always looking for us to encourage one another and partner with Him for the sake of the Kingdom of God. Of course, this means we need to be ready and filled to over-flowing and sensitive to the Holy Spirit at all times! Much as Ananias found it really difficult... at least he went!!! The Lord then shared and explained to him just how important Saul was going to be... how he was destined as a chosen vessel to carry His Name before the Gentiles and kings and the descendants of Israel. No-one else knew these secrets at this time! But The Holy Spirit shared these treasures with Ananias and he became a prophetic carrier for the Lord to Saul who was still in darkness! Oh WOW!!!

That is SO wonderful that God could so change Ananias' heart to see this murderer and terrorist as a "Brother in Christ!" It was so amazing too... how The Spirit revealed what had happened when Saul had his divine encounter on the Damascus road. I am full of admiration as I see this ordinary faithful man pop into Scripture and how he was the one God chose to lay his hands on Saul and see him filled with the Holy Spirit... and THEN the miracle of something like scales fell from Saul's eyes and he recovered his sight!! We don't know any more about Ananias... but he left his mark and **deposited his treasures** to a man who would later write three quarters of the New Testament... Hallelujah!! That is quite a legacy!

Saul received the Treasures of Darkness?

The Bible tells us that Saul proclaimed Jesus as the Son of God immediately in the synagogues and suddenly all the Scriptures he knew from studying the Laws of God in his past came alive with Truth and he just couldn't keep quiet!! We are told Saul's power increased greatly as he became more and more proficient in proving that Jesus was the Anointed Messiah... and everyone was astonished!

Saul had had no idea what treasures were in him, neither did anyone else!

BUT GOD had hidden "The Treasures of Darkness" even in a terrorist!

So, Saul became the Apostle Paul and he spent his whole life giving all the treasures away to all of us who love the Word of God so that we can,

"Dare to Receive the Treasures of Darkness!"

Chapter 22.

Treasures in Prison for PETER and JOHN!

Matthew 25:31-40 Jesus, very near the end of His ministry, was teaching about when the Son of Man would come in His glory and all the holy angels of God with Him and that He would be sitting on the Throne of His glory. That is when the King will say, "Come, you blessed of My Father, inherit the kingdom prepared for you from the foundation of the world. For I was hungry and you gave Me food, I was thirsty and you gave Me something to drink, I was a stranger and you brought Me together with yourselves and welcomed Me, I was naked and you clothed Me, I was sick and you visited Me, I was in prison and you came to see Me".

Then the just and upright will answer Him, "Lord, when did we see you hungry and give you food, or thirsty and gave you something to drink? And when did we see you a stranger and welcomed you, or naked and clothed you? And when did we see you sick or in prison and came to visit you?" And the King will reply to them...

"Truly I tell you in as far as you did it for one of the least you did it for me."

Soon after Jesus spoke these words... I noticed that was when Judas Iscariot went to the chief priests to arrange for Jesus to be arrested and he was paid thirty pieces of silver to look for an opportunity to betray Jesus. I thought about this and wondered how this may have triggered such an evil response of betrayal from Judas Iscariot? Then I re-read the passage again and v 45 might be the key: Jesus said, "Solemnly I declare to you, **in so far as you failed to do it for the least, you failed to do it for Me**".

It is possible that Judas had his own selective hearing that day! Did he realize he would be punished for what he hadn't done!?? Would he be recognised as a thief! We know he kept the purse and maybe at that point he suddenly realized that he would be found out for what he should not have done and had failed to do! When a thief thinks he is going to be found out, there can be an irrational response as the powers of darkness are confronted with truth.

This thought comes to me through an experience that happened when we were at Bible College... It was discovered that someone was stealing the letters that arrived to bless the ministry and so money and cheques were discovered to have been stolen. This all came into the light as the Director publicly informed all of us students that someone was a thief among us.

You can imagine the atmosphere!! One student started to confess, "I must be the thief!" However, this proved to be completely wrong... as a trap was laid to catch the real thief a couple of days later! But it turned out that the student who thought it must have been him was convicted by the lies of the enemy because he had an issue that had not been dealt with in his own life. What I am trying to say is that when light confronts darkness, there will always be a reaction to hide or to be propelled into a greater degree of darkness instigated by the work of the evil one.

Maybe Jesus was trying to warn Judas even then? I don't know! But it is certainly true that whatever we do for the least we are doing for Jesus and whatever we fail to do, we fail to do it for Jesus... and there will be consequences!

I want to share about my own prison experiences!
Visiting prisons and preaching to people in prison was not at all on my agenda until the Holy Spirit opened that particular door of ministry for me a few years back! I don't know why, but I kind of assumed, that it would be women's prison... so I was quite surprised that it turned out to be a high security men's prison! I had never encountered such rigorous searching in my life or so many locked doors to go through! My remit was to preach for forty minutes and I was allowed to give an appeal for Salvation at the end. The prisoners were free to choose to come to the meeting or not, as they chose... but there were armed guards all long the back row keeping an eye in case anything got out of hand!

I had been told specifically not to ask what crimes they were imprisoned for and not to touch the men at all... My first visit went fine as I shared my testimony and I went away really encouraged as two of the prisoners responded and gave their hearts to Jesus! My second visit was quite a different challenge as there were three men near the back who had obviously come to the meeting to specifically cause a disruption! I concentrated my gaze away from them and continued sharing the Gospel... always wise!! As I came to the end and gave the invitation for those who wanted to respond and give their lives to Jesus... I was absolutely staggered to see the main culprit who was causing the disruption running down to the front and weeping on his knees as he repented of his sins!

But what I didn't know, until six months later when I was visiting the prison again, was how the Holy Spirit had been dramatically at work during that particular meeting. Yes, those three prisoners had come specifically to cause problems... but apparently as I was preaching, the Lord spoke personally to this one young man saying, "What this lady is speaking is the truth and this is your final opportunity to be saved, forgiven, and have the gift of eternal life. I am Jesus and I do not want you to go to hell".

WOW!!!

So when I returned to that same prison six months later, this particular man, I will call him Terry, gave his testimony, which is how I know exactly what happened that night as he ran weeping down to the front to surrender his life at the foot of the Cross and receive his forgiveness!!! Oh, isn't it amazing how the Lord loves every sinner no matter what they have done! The Cross works for all who come humbling themselves and putting faith in Jesus Christ as Saviour and Lord!

What a **"Treasure of Darkness"** Terry turned out to be as he led many Bible Studies in the prison and evangelized many of the inmates! He became an incredible soul winner for the Lord there in prison!!

That same evening on my third visit, the Holy Spirit whispered to me: Ask how many in the meeting are murderers? I tried to ignore it as I knew this was not the proper protocol! But I have always said, Lord "I will be obedient" ... so eventually that is what I asked!! Immediately there was an atmosphere to say the least... and no-one said anything, they were all just looking at each other... they knew the rules!! Now my heart was pounding and again the Holy Spirit said to me: "Put your hand up Gill and confess that you are a murderer and the only difference is that you know you are forgiven." So, I did this, while the men in the meeting gasped, I confessed publicly that I had murdered Jesus Christ the Son of God with my adultery. Then I invited any of them who knew they were a convicted murderer to put their hands up. I was absolutely taken aback as sixteen men put their hands up and one by one, they rushed weeping to the front asking to be forgiven! Jesus loves those in prison, and it was a tremendous privilege to see those lives completely transformed. In Luke 4:18 Jesus said, "The Spirit of the Lord is upon me, He has anointed me to be hope for the poor, freedom for the broken-hearted, and new eyes for the blind, and to preach to prisoners... you are set free"!

Such beautiful unexpected "Treasures of Darkness" in a prison!!

PETER and JOHN in Prison

Acts 4:3 Peter and John were put in prison after the wonderful miracle of healing the lame man at the Gate Beautiful when another 2000 people had come to faith in Jesus Christ who had been raised from the dead!

"The officials laid hands on them and unfairly put them in prison."

The next day it was Peter who boldly spoke up in v 10 "Let it be known and understood by all of you, and by the whole house of Israel, that in the name and through the power and authority of Jesus Christ of Nazareth, whom you crucified, but whom God raised from the dead, in Him and by means of Him this man is standing here before you well and sound in body". v12 "There is salvation in and through no one else, for there is no other name under heaven among men by which we must be saved."

Peter and John were faithful to proclaim the Gospel even in prison.

What amazed the officials was the eloquence of these ordinary men and they recognised that they had been with Jesus! They tried to forbid them to preach about Jesus... but Peter and John replied, "Is it right in the sight of God to listen to you and obey you rather than God? But we cannot help telling what we have seen and heard". And they had to let them go!!

What "Treasures of Darkness" did they experience?

When the rulers and council members had further threatened them and because the man who had been healed was standing there... **they let them go free!** So, they went back to their own company of believers... they were all together in wonderful unity and extolled the Lord God Almighty. Then they all lifted up their voices in one accord praying: v 29-33 "Now, Lord, observe their threats and grant to your bond servants full freedom to declare your message fearlessly, while You stretch out Your hand to cure and perform signs and wonders through the authority and by the power of the name of your holy Servant Jesus".

And immediately when they had prayed, the place was shaken; and they were all filled with the Holy Spirit and they continued to speak the Word of God with freedom and boldness and courage. Now the company of believers were of one heart and mind, everything they had was in common and for the use of all. And with great strength and ability and power the apostles delivered their testimony to the resurrection of the Lord Jesus, and great grace and favour rested richly upon them all.

This was a second mighty empowering by the Holy Spirit! That is a wonderful "Treasure of Darkness"!

Now it is hopefully very unlikely that we might land up in an actual prison!! But we do need to be encouraged by the example of Peter and John and learn and see the reward of **"The Treasures of Darkness"** that came from heaven, not just for them, but for the whole company of believers! This prison experience inaugurated a new season for everyone. Generosity was overwhelming as they all were filled again with the Holy Spirit as the Lord was poured out upon them in such power. There was a new oneness, a new community spirit, a new boldness and new courage and immense favour rested upon them all.

Hallelujah!!

However, prison can be experienced in many different ways for us as individuals... a difficult abusive marriage, the torment of mental health issues, the pain of losing a loved one or a sudden debilitating illness... any kind of confinement can seem like a prison sentence and can affect any of us at some time in our lives and there always seems to be no way out! This sort of prison is an internal experience that is SO painful and constricting. Perhaps your Lockdown experience has seemed like that? I know it did to me until the Holy Spirit urged me to start writing this book!

But I want you to know that Jesus Christ is there right alongside you as He is with me... it is the Holy Spirit's Presence that produces treasures in whatever constrained situation you might find yourself in. I promise you that there can be **"Treasures of Darkness"** waiting for you, simply because the Word of God has made that promise and He is always such a good, good Father and deeply cares for each one of us as His own beloved children!

To demonstrate just what a caring Father He is... I would like to share a true story with you... Some of you may have heard of Mahesh Chavda? We had the privilege at one of the Good News Crusade Camps as Team members of watching him minister for several hours at a meeting for about 300 very sick children. He had SO much compassion and love flowing through his ministry that I had never witnessed before. This very deeply impacted me! Later I discovered how this amazing ministry of healing and power in the love and compassion of Christ had been developed at a very special time in his life.

Apparently, Mahesh was led by the Holy Spirit to go into a women's mental institution where there was a group of women who were completely out of their minds in a padded cell. The Lord had him sit down on the very dirty floor among the women and continuously sing over and over again, "Jesus loves me this I know for the Bible tells me so!" There seemed to be no response at all, but he continued going in each week for six months or it may have been even longer! All the time he was only singing that same little chorus over and over again for about an hour as the Holy Spirit instructed him.

But one day after several months as he was singing again... this time one young woman drew up close to sit by him and started singing with him... it was the first sign of the Holy Spirit getting through!! Gradually there was a complete shift in the atmosphere as the Holy Spirit brought the manifested Presence of the Risen Saviour into that padded cell. One by one each of those demented women came through for Jesus and each one was restored back into their right minds! Their prison doors of darkness were opened ... Hallelujah! They were all healed in their minds as the light and love of Christ came bursting in and apparently each one of these women became a living testimony to the saving and delivering love and power of Jesus!! Mahesh certainly received a very special compassionate anointing through that experience which he now shares all over the world!

No prison can withhold "The Treasures of Darkness" when Jesus walks in!

I believe that we should all take heart and see that we, as individuals, are going to come out of this Lockdown with new treasures to give away to others! We shall all be different and exhibiting much more of the fruit of the Spirit as we connect with people! We shall experience a New Season, a New Mantle, a New Magnificent Out-pouring of the Holy Spirit, and a

Tremendous In-gathering of an unequalled, never before seen, Harvest for the Kingdom of God... that should send us running after God with more and more hunger!! Oh, Beloved reader we must all keep treasure hunting!

New "Treasures of Darkness" are to be gleaned... AND at this unprecedented time there are Hidden Riches of Secret Places!

Get ready...your confinement might have seemed like a type of prison... but personally I am determined to come out with such tremendous treasures!

Chapter 23

Supernatural Messengers bring Treasures to PETER!

Acts 12:1-17 The Passion Translation, Herod incited persecution against the church, causing great harm to the believers. He even had the apostle James, John's brother, beheaded. When Herod realized how much this pleased the Jewish leaders, he had Peter arrested and thrown into prison during the Feast of Passover. Sixteen soldiers were assigned to guard him until Herod could bring him to public trial immediately after the Passover celebrations were over.

The church went into a season of intense intercession, asking God to free him.

The night before Herod planned to bring him to trial, he made sure that Peter was securely bound with two chains. Peter was sound asleep between two soldiers, with additional guards stationed outside his cell door, when all at once an angel of the Lord appeared, filling his prison cell with a brilliant light. The angel struck Peter on the side to awaken him and said, "Hurry up! Let's go! Instantly the chains fell off his wrists. The angel told him, "Get dressed, put on you sandals, bring your cloak, and follow me".

Peter quickly left his cell and followed the angel, even though he thought it was only a dream or a vision, for it seemed so unreal... he couldn't believe it was really happening! They walked unseen past the first guard post and then the second before coming to the iron-gate that leads to the city... and the gate swung open all by itself right in front of them!

They went out into the city and were walking down a narrow street when, all of a sudden, the angel disappeared. That was when Peter realized that he wasn't having a dream! He said to himself, "This is really happening! The Lord sent an angel to rescue me from the clutches of Herod and from what the Jewish leaders planned to do to me".

When he realized this, he decided to go to the house of Mary and her son John Mark. The house was filled with people praying. When he knocked on the door to the courtyard, a young servant girl named Rhoda got up to see who it was. When she recognised Peter's voice, she was so excited that she forgot to open the door, but ran back inside the house to announce, "Peter is standing outside!"

"Are you crazy?"They said to her, but when she kept insisting, they answered "Well it must be his angel." Meanwhile, Peter was still outside, knocking on the door. When they finally opened it, they were shocked to find Peter standing there. He signalled for them to be quiet as he shared with them the miraculous way the Lord brought him out of prison!!

An angel led Peter to freedom, what a "Treasure of Darkness"!

The first thing I noticed was that there was an evil plot against Peter... But we need to believe that **whatever evil scheme might come against us that it can never prevent God's plan for our lives as we trust in Him!** Jesus told the disciples in John 16:32-33 "An hour is coming... in the world you will have tribulation and trials and distress and frustration; but be of good cheer, take courage; be confident, certain, undaunted! For I have overcome the world. I have deprived it of power to harm you and have conquered it for you".

The next thing I noticed is that Peter was supported by people outside fervently praying together in unison. We always need people who will support us in covering prayer!! **The Lord answers the prayers of the saints... even if it's at the eleventh hour!** They may have thought that their payers had not been heard because Peter was still in prison and his execution would be the following day... **BUT GOD!** The people did not give up and went on interceding for Peter and his release. Teach us Oh Lord not to stop praying... even till the last minute!!

Fervent prayer releases angelic forces into our atmosphere! "Treasures of Darkness" are revealed!

Then I looked at Peter... he was sleeping soundly between two soldiers; he was in chains with four squads of soldiers of four each to guard him. **Peter was in the utter darkness of the prison, but he was at complete peace!!** That is God's supernatural grace of Christ available for each one of us in whatever dark and difficult circumstances we might find ourselves in! ... we should be expecting that same grace abounding to us!!! Yes, and it reminded me that it was just like Jesus as He slept in the boat in the storm! Bless him, Peter had learnt from the Master! When we can sleep in peace in the midst of the storm or darkness... then the atmosphere is ready to be invaded by heaven's resources!! Hallelujah!!

Next, the angel of the Lord arrived filling the dark prison cell with a brilliant light. Wherever we may find ourselves, **the light of Christ is ready to come flooding into our situation**... because Colossians 1:27 "Christ IN us is our hope of Glory!" Jesus is The Light and when His Presence fills us then we will experience His light wherever we may be... and the angel touched Peter and said, "Get up quickly!"

THEN the chains fell off Peter!

When freedom comes to us supernaturally it can almost feel like a dream! The angel spoke more instructions to Peter, and he obeyed and followed the angel. The Lord kept all the guards asleep as they passed by the first and second guards and then even the iron-gate just swung open without any help! I am telling you, my dear precious reader, there can be no obstacle that can stand in the way when the Spirit of Freedom is sent from heaven to liberate us from the darkness of our prison.

It was only when the angel disappeared that Peter realized it was really happening and not a dream! Real freedom may take time for us to experience in our human senses... but it absolutely real as the Bible says in 2 Corinthians 3:17 **"Where the Spirit of the Lord is there is Liberty"**! Yes, even those faithful praying saints could hardly believe when they saw Peter at the door!! Open our eyes Lord!!

Angelic messengers are sent to reveal those "Treasures of Darkness"

PAUL and SILAS: Paul had a supernatural vision during the night when a man from Macedonia appeared before him, pleading with him to come over into Macedonia to help them. Earlier the Holy Spirit had forbidden them to go into the province of Asia and also not to go into Bithynia. But this new vision gave them confidence that God had called them to proclaim the glad tidings of the Gospel in Macedonia, so Paul and Silas duly arrived in Philippi. The Holy Spirit confirmed that they were in the centre of God's will as the Lord went ahead of them and they met a very special lady called Lydia whose heart the Lord opened to accept the Lord Jesus Christ as her personal Saviour and Messiah. This was a divine connection that produced much fruit. Then she and all her household were baptized, and she invited Paul and Silas to stay in her house.

These are beautiful "Treasures of Darkness"!

It is always wonderfully encouraging when we see the Holy Spirit going before us... but sometimes the enemy also has plans to disrupt things! We see how this happened here in this chapter; as Paul and Silas were on their way to the place of prayer, they encountered a young slave girl who had an evil spirit of divination, the spirit of Python. As a fortune-teller she made great profits for her owners! We read that day after day she followed them shouting... "These men are servants of the Great High God, and they are telling us how to be saved".

It was true BUT the wrong source!!

Finally, we are told that Paul got annoyed and turned and spoke directly to the spirit indwelling her, "I command you in the name of Jesus, the Anointed One, to come out of her now". At that very moment, the spirit came out of her and all her evil powers disappeared, so much so that her slave owners started accusing Paul and Silas and had them dragged before the authorities.

Paul and Silas find themselves in a secure prison!

Acts 16: 22-40 "A great crowd gathered... the Roman officials ordered Paul and Silas to be stripped of their garments and beaten with rods on their bare backs. After they were severely beaten, they were thrown into prison and the jailer was commanded to guard them securely. So, the jailer placed them in the innermost cell of the prison with their feet bound and chained.

Paul and Silas, undaunted, were praying in the middle of the night and sang songs of praise to God, while all the other prisoners listened to their worship. Suddenly, a great earthquake shook the foundations of the prison. All at once every prison door flung open and the chains of all the prisoners came loose. Startled, the jailer awoke and saw every cell door standing open. He assumed that all the prisoners had escaped so he drew his sword and was about to kill himself when Paul shouted in the darkness:

"Stop... Don't hurt yourself. We are all still here!"

The jailer called for a light. When he saw that they were all in their cells, he rushed in and fell trembling at their feet. Then he led Paul and Silas outside and asked, **"What must I do to be saved?"**. They answered, "Believe in the Lord Jesus and you will be saved... you and all your family".

Even though the hour was late, he washed their wounds. Then he and all his family were baptized. He took Paul and Silas into his own home and set them at his table and fed them. The jailer and all his family were filled with joy in their newfound faith in God.

What "Treasures of Darkness" were experienced that day!

At daybreak, the magistrates sent officers to the prison with orders to tell the jailer, "Let those two men go". The jailer informed Paul and Silas. "The magistrates have sent orders to release you. So, you are free to go now." But Paul told the officers, "Look, they had us beaten in public, without a fair trial... and we are Roman citizens. Do you think we're just going to quietly walk away after they threw us in prison and violated all our rights? Absolutely not! You go back and tell the magistrates that they need to come down here themselves and escort us out!"

When the officers went back and reported what Paul and Silas had told them, the magistrates were frightened, especially upon hearing that they had beaten two Roman citizens without due process. So, they went to the prison and apologized to Paul and Silas, begging them repeatedly saying, "Please leave our city". So, Paul and Silas left prison and went back to Lydia's house, where they met the believers and encouraged them before departing.

As I have looked at this Scripture, I realize that The Lord has no problem working in the darkness! Sometimes we might feel that the situation is too difficult for even the Almighty God to handle! We are wrong! Remember, The Lord is an expert at working in the darkness and has promised that there are **"Treasures of Darkness"** waiting for us!! He does some of His best work when it is especially dark!!

With Peter, God sent an angel, with Paul and Silas it was an earthquake!

The means of release may be different, but the result was similar –**FREEDOM!!** The prison could not hold them! With Peter and with Paul and Silas they were all innocent and unfairly put in jail, yet they maintained their peace in the darkness of the prison. The Holy Spirit empowered them to have that supernatural peace and the special grace they needed in their circumstances. That should encourage us that The Presence of the Lord can do the same for us whenever we may need it.

Expect the Unexpected!

Peter slept... Paul and Silas prayed and worshipped... in BOTH circumstances they were witnesses of Jesus Christ and their lives would have radiated the Presence of God with them and, clearly, they would have been seen to be entirely different to the other prisoners! On neither of the occasions did they know how the Lord would set them free... but they were assured that He would!! That assurance needs to be ours too! Be careful that fear, anxieties or worries do not take hold of us when we feel hemmed in... fears restrict the working of the Holy Spirit on our behalf.

Psalm 4:1

"You freed me when I was hemmed in and enlarged me when I was in distress."

Think what wonderful testimonies we can have when The Lord delivers us! We do not need to panic but be assured and confident that the Lord will work in the darkness so that we come out with treasures and riches from those secret places. No wonder it says in Revelation 12:11 "They overcome the enemy by means of the blood of the Lamb and by the word of their testimony and did not love their own lives even in the face of death".

I believe that Peter, Paul and Silas, on these two different occasions, had overcome the enemy right there in the prison before the actual release happened. That can be our experience too as we stand on the Word: 1 John 4:4 "He who is in you is greater than he who is in the world". Jesus demonstrated that victory for us in the garden of Gethsemane before He endured the Cross!! Our victory does not come from outside, but all the power of the Risen Lord Jesus that is IN us as Born Again believers.

Each dark situation is an opportunity to prove His power at work within us.

Ephesians 1:19-20 "And so that you can know and understand what is the immeasurable and unlimited and surpassing greatness of His power in and for us who believe, as demonstrated in the working of His mighty strength which He exerted in Christ when He raised Him from the dead and seated Him at His own right hand in the heavenly places. Far above all rule and authority and power and dominion and every name that is named, not only in this world but also in the age and the world which are

150

to come."

**Precious one...we need a continuing increased revelation of this great power
IN us and FOR us!**

"Dare to Receive the Treasures of Darkness"

Chapter 24.

Treasures of Darkness in Real Life... PERSONAL EXPERIENCES!

In the most impossible or difficult situations... God has ways of bringing Heaven's Supernatural powers into our world as we stand unshaken on the Promises of God in His Word. These are often the most beautiful **"Treasures of Darkness"** that can tend to slip by without us even recognising them, or worse, not appreciating them... just because we are focusing on the darkness and not the treasures!

Oh, Holy Spirit we need your help all the time!

I am sure that each of us has a testimony that illustrates just how God has brought us through many of life's challenges supernaturally. I want to encourage you with three of my own experiences... so that you can step out in faith trusting that the Lord has magnificent treasures stored up for you too!

There have been times when the Holy Spirit has asked to do something that my flesh has not wanted to do, or that there has seemed no logical reason to be immediately obedient... that is often where we need to take a risk, step out and keep our focus steadfastly on Jesus!! A bit like Peter when he stepped out of the boat in the storm simply on the word... **"Come!"**

It was just like that one night several years ago...

While I was enjoying the wonderful worship at Spring Harvest and I was deeply engaged with the Holy Spirit in singing my heart out to my Beloved Jesus... unexpectedly He spoke to me! "I want you to go home tonight." Skippy was not yet a Christian and had allowed me to have a whole week there and I was really enjoying myself! So, leaving early was not on my agenda as there was another full day of teaching and an evening of anointed worship still left of the week and I was really hungry for more of the teaching and building up in this great anointed atmosphere.

BUT GOD had other plans!!

I stayed to the very last minute but at about 11.40 p.m. I collected my things and headed for the car to start the journey from Prestatyn in North Wales to Aberystwyth where we lived at the time. However, I had forgotten that my petrol tank was more or less on empty... so I hastily made my way to the nearest Petrol Station only to find that it was closed and so were all the other places! Now here was my dilemma... had I really heard from the Holy Spirit? Or had I imagined it? If it was the Holy Spirit that had spoken to me, how was I going to get petrol to drive about one hundred miles? I was convinced, after praying, that I had heard God's voice and so I decided I would start on the journey in obedience and trust God!

It was about mid-night when I eventually started on the journey home... I started the engine and glanced at the petrol dial... EMPTY! Then my heart literally leapt for joy as I watched the dial indicator move before my eyes. One moment it was on empty and now the gauge was registering FULL!! Wow! This was a totally unexpected **"Treasure of Darkness"**! I realized that the Lord must have filled up the tank supernaturally for me and I can tell you I really praised, I sang loudly and worshipped all the way until I got to a place called Bala which was still about fifty miles to go. As I stopped at the traffic lights in Bala, to my horror I saw that the petrol gauge now was back to empty! But, somehow, I knew in my spirit that my Lord was not going to abandon me... but how was He going to help me out of this hopeless situation???

It was a very dark night with no moon or stars at all...

I should have known that God is always in control! Almost immediately to my amazement the Holy Spirit began to speak to me as He gave me explicit instructions to turn first right at the next traffic lights, then take the first left down a country road and then two miles further on to turn down a small lane second on my left. It really was an adventure...

Picture the situation... I am in completely dark territory with no lighting on these small roads and I haven't a clue where I am or where I am going... except that I was following the voice of the Holy Spirit! On my right I noticed that there were fields with a low hedge and on my left were rather large houses back from the road. Suddenly, the Lord said, "Stop here" ... I stopped opposite a gravel drive on my left-hand side... there was a large house quite a way back from the small lane and there were tall bushes on either side. If you can imagine, I was sitting in the car feeling a bit of a fool, yet excited in a strange way... when I distinctly heard the

153

crunching of the gravel down the drive as a man in a helmet came walking toward me with a petrol can in his right hand and he said to me, "Here is the petrol you need Gill" and he proceeded to take off the petrol cap and pour in the petrol!

An Angel brought the "Treasures of Darkness" this time!

To say I was staggered is a complete understatement and when I looked to say "Thank you" ... this stranger had completely vanished! I was trembling, shaking and yet aware of this awesome Presence of God with me. Then I realized I had no idea how to get back on to the main road to Aberystwyth from where I was!! Thankfully the Holy Spirit had mercy on me, and He guided me back the way I had come and soon I was on the main road and driving through the market town of Machynlleth before finally I arrived at our home in Aberystwyth. I was praying in the Spirit all the way and worshipping out loud as I drove those last fifty miles.

As Skippy was not expecting me, I let myself in as quietly as possible and crept upstairs to our bedroom... it must have been the one loose floorboard on the landing that woke him up! He sat bolt upright and at first he thought I was an intruder but as he put the light on and saw it was me, he said, "What are you doing here? You were not coming back till tomorrow!" My answer was, "Oh Darling I am so sorry but the Lord spoke to me to come back tonight and I had no means of letting you know and I really didn't mean to wake you up at this unearthly hour in the morning... please forgive me".

Then Skippy, half awake, looked at the bedside clock and said, "I don't know what you are talking about its only 12.15 a.m. and we can still have a good night's sleep!" That is what really blew my mind... I crumpled on to my knees and sobbed out loud... "It is impossible I only left Prestatyn at about 12.00 a.m. ... your clock must be wrong." But NO... the clock wasn't wrong! Then, to my amazement, Skippy just turned over and went back to sleep while I was still completely overcome and trembling with the incredible Presence of the Lord Himself!

It took me ages before I fully realized the enormity of what had happened! The Lord had not only provided the petrol supernaturally in the car, but He had arranged for an Angel to deliver petrol to me personally AND THEN TO TOP IT ALL... He had also transported me one hundred miles in about 15 minutes! WOW!!!

That night Heaven invaded earth with "Treasures of Darkness!"

The next testimony I want to share with you is one that brought a different kind of **"Treasures of Darkness"** into my life as well as to others in a very outstanding way! I had arranged to take Sarah Watkins with me to Jamaica... it was her very first Mission trip abroad! Many will know that more recently I have handed over my Conferences to her after working and travelling together for many years! Although, sadly, this year everything has had to be cancelled due to the Corona Virus! However, on this occasion as it was her first trip abroad, so we arranged to meet up at the Premier Inn at Heathrow the night before. We didn't know each other very well but found out the next morning that we are both very early and punctual people and duly arrived to check in with plenty of time to spare. I thought it was rather odd that we were the only ones there... only to find out from the Air Jamaica Official that our flight had been cancelled!

Not good news at all... especially as I was preaching the next morning in a Conference in Montego Bay in Jamaica! Not a good way to begin a Mission... I explained our predicament and we were told to wait, and they would get back to us. In a very short time, the Air Jamaica Official came back and assured us they would get us on a flight that afternoon to New York, put us up in a Five Star Hotel and fly us on to Montego Bay in the morning in time for the Conference! Needless to say, we were greatly relieved, and we were especially very grateful as they gave us several vouchers for food while we waited for our flight later on! In fact, we were treated exceptionally well!

"Unexpected... Treasures of Darkness!"

We were told that the reason they were able to do all this for us was because we were so early coming to check in! A real blessing!! This was a fabulous provision and Sarah and I were able to relax until our flight was called later that afternoon. We didn't see much of New York, but we certainly had five-star treatment and accommodation!! Yes! The airline did as they had promised, and we arrived in Montego Bay on time and had many amazing meetings where the Lord poured out His Spirit in power! We were extremely grateful for the Lord's provision and kept praising God for the way He had looked after us so well!

However, it was a few weeks later, after we arrived back, that Sarah contacted me to give me details of even more wonderful **"Treasures of Darkness"**! What I had not realized was that Sarah had previously asked the Holy Spirit to prove to her husband Mark that the Lord would provide for this Mission Trip! The news she gave me that day was that Air Jamaica had completely refunded all of our costs for the whole trip... both our outward and return flights! WOW!!!

These were totally unprecedented and unexpected "Treasures of Darkness"!

I really want to encourage you so that you may believe that our Father in Heaven always has surprising treasures to pour into our lives as we step out in obedience to partner with the Holy Spirit! This is the adventure of walking by faith and not by sight! I am overcome with the goodness of God... He knows exactly how to encourage us! The path He asks us to follow is a path of resurrection life which is such an honour to travel with Him. All along the way there are unlimited treasures popping up before us, with us or behind us...

How precious O Lord is your unfailing love!

The Glory of His Presence protects us, provides for us, and overshadows us. Even in the darkest seasons, as we cling to the Lord there is the fragrance and touch of the Holy Spirit personally resting upon our lives. God knows exactly how to inspire us, comfort us and give us hope in those difficult unexpected circumstances... and He gives us divine wisdom from above!! What a magnificent Lord God Almighty He is!!!

I want to say that our God is far bigger than you or I can ever imagine, and, in these days, we need to ask the Holy Spirit to enlarge our vision of Who God is. The Lord is the giver of great visions... so we need to ask Him!! Vision sparks the fire and passion within us and enables us and moves us onward towards our destiny in spite of any obstacles or darkness that might be standing in the way.

I read the other day... "Great vision always precedes great achievement!"
SO true!!

On one occasion I was lying on the beach sharing an intimate moment with the Lord when the Holy Spirit spoke to me, "Get up Gill, look out to sea and tell me what you see?" Almost reluctantly I got up, the beach was deserted as it was very early in the morning... I told the Lord that as I looked out to sea, I could see a sailing boat about six miles offshore. I was not expecting His reply, "Gill I want you to swim to that boat". Now my natural mind kicked in as I answered, "BUT Lord it's a very long way and I am not a very good swimmer and the beach is deserted". However, I have discovered that the Holy Spirit does not explain things, he just wants obedience!!

So, I began to walk towards the water, it was absolutely calm. My eyes were focused on the boat, it seemed so far away... first my toes, then my ankles, then my knees, then up to my waist and almost immediately I was up to my neck as I was on tiptoe!! Then suddenly I couldn't feel the bottom and I began to swim towards the boat for what seemed like ages as I fixed my eyes on the sailing boat! Then I made a big mistake... I stopped swimming and looked back!! Not a good idea as I saw I was about a couple of miles from the shore and fear took hold of me. I began treading water and I said, "Jesus, I am so sorry, would you mind if I didn't go any further?" To my delight He answered, "No, Gill that is alright, I am so pleased with you for going this far towards the boat!" I literally felt the Lord's smile of approval!

But then I realized I was too tired to swim back and so I asked The Lord, "How am I going to get back?" To which He replied, "Gill, just lie on your back relax in my love and float and begin to praise me"! It seemed strange... but that is what I did! That was when the **"Treasures of Darkness"** arrived as I suddenly felt my head touch the sand on the shore!! Yes! It was a miracle... but I have learnt that the Holy Spirit always wants us to gain the most from every situation and absorb the treasures so that we can grow deeper in love with Jesus and understand the bigness of our God and how he operates!! Then we will have unlimited treasures to give away!!

As I marvelled and pondered over what had just happened... I asked what the Holy Spirit wanted to teach me. To which He replied:

"Gill, your vision must always be bigger than you could ever do yourself."

So, I want to give you a few guide lines:

1) Vision comes from God He alone knows what you or I are capable of and the gifts He has given us. Vision should not be limited to ourselves or even our own lifetime... we need to look towards leaving a legacy for others to go further than we have been. I love this phrase, "Our

ceiling should be someone else's platform!"

2) Vision comes out of our past experiences and is influenced by the people that God has put around us! Be a person who encourages others and believe in them! I would not be where I am today if the Lord had not put people around me who believed in me... for which I am eternally grateful!

3) Vision meets other people's needs... A God-given vision goes far beyond what one person can accomplish. It should bless others and it will include other people alongside us to enable the vision to be fulfilled.

4) Vision attracts resources... it is a bit like a magnet that draws people, it has definite challenges and yet it unites people who catch the vision! The greater your vision the more faith-filled people you will attract, and you will need their help to facilitate it!

5) Vision... you will need to fight for your vision in spite of the obstacles or blockages...

KEEP FOCUSED and KEEP MOVING and KEEP BELIEVING!!

Vision releases "Treasures of Darkness!"

Chapter 25

Treasures from the Book of JOB

THE PROMISE: Isaiah 60:1-2 "Arise from the depression and prostration in which circumstances have kept you...**Rise to a new life!** Shine, be radiant with the glory of the Lord, for your light has come, and the glory of the Lord has risen upon you! For behold, darkness shall cover the earth, and dense darkness all peoples, **but the Lord shall arise upon you and His glory will be seen on you.**"

Many people are mentioning this Scripture during these days and I want to team it up with the subject of this book from Isaiah 45:3 **"I will give you the Treasures of Darkness and Hidden Riches of**

secret places". To pretend that there is no darkness to me seems very unrealistic... because the Holy Spirit clearly recognises that circumstances in our lives do cause darkness! Personally, I do not believe that it is Godly or spiritual to ignore the difficulties, challenges and darkness all around us... but we must certainly not dwell on them... but look for God's treasures that are promised to us!

However, I do believe that we need to know how to respond and let the Word of God teach us that darkness is not something to be afraid of when we belong to our Heavenly Father. Most of all, as I have said, we need to keep seeking for **"The Treasures of Darkness"** in every situation that we might find ourselves in... the treasures are there for us! Open our eyes Lord!!! Our Heavenly Father is wonderful at rewarding His children!

God can use darkness to develop the character of Christ in our lives!

The call to us all at this time is: **ARISE to a New Life!** We are not meant to be under the circumstances: In the Bible, Colossians 3:1-3 says, "If then you have been raised with Christ to a new life, thus sharing His resurrection from the dead, aim at and **seek the rich eternal treasures that are above**, where Christ is seated at the right hand of God. And set your minds and keep them set on what is above, the higher things, not on the things that are on the earth. For as far as this world is concerned you have died, and your new life is hidden with Christ in God".

There are Eternal Treasures to be received!

How do we receive them? We need to put our whole faith and total trust in the promises of God! As we have seen in 2 Corinthians 1:20 "ALL the promises of God are: Yes and Amen in Christ Jesus!" It's called seeing things from God's perspective where His light has come, and the glory of the Lord has risen upon you and His glory is promised to be seen on you according to His Word! Jesus tells us that He has given us His glory in John 17:22 "I have given to them the glory and honour which you have given me".

Receive this treasure of God's Perspective!

This is called walking by faith and not by sight! As long as the Word shows me the Truth ... I am happy to believe and trust in whatever it says, even if I am not yet personally experiencing it in my own life. That is when I am inspired to go treasure hunting with the Holy Spirit, and I make a decision to allow Him complete freedom in my life to dig out or put in different treasures that I might not be aware of! It is my way of totally surrendering to Jesus again and again!

So, in this final CHAPTER of **"Treasures of Darkness"** I want to share a few glimpses of insight from the book of Job! Everyone knows he experienced the worse sort of darkness, loss, tragedy and even sickness ending up among the ashes. **BUT GOD**... that was not the end of the story! If we are really humble and open enough, we will be able to understand a little more of just what marvellous treasures God gave to Job out of the midst of his terrible darkness.

Nothing is eternally more important than a New Revelation of God Himself!

As I have read the Bible recently, I have become acutely aware that often we do not get a new deeper intimacy and revelation of God **UNTIL**... we see the utter imperfections and truth about ourselves! The darkness Job experienced brought him into a far greater revelation of Who God was... losing all his worldly riches, his family, his friends, and even his health left him with utter dependency on the Lord!

But we must remember that it wasn't God that hurt Job... God's plan was twice as many blessings!

Looking at the principles here, it is absolutely true that we need to hold all of these things in our lives and our relationships very lightly... because we are not entitled to own them... they are God's gifts to us! They are blessings for us to appreciate! We need to treasure the good things we have been blessed with! But they must never become more important than our relationship with the Lord.

But even in Job's darkness and tragedy, God had already prepared and stored up for Job a double portion of treasures. This all happened WHEN Job saw himself in the light of God's holiness and awesome power. Most new revelations come after the Holy Spirit works in the deep secret places of darkness.

These are the hidden riches of secret places!

A bit like a caterpillar's process of transformation when it is out of sight in the cocoon before the beautiful butterfly is released into its destiny of a new life! Inside that cocoon there is a tremendous struggle in the darkness hidden away that will ensure that there will be a total change and transformation on the inside and that happens away from the light!! Similarly, the Lord is so careful with each one of us and He alone knows what pressures are needed to bring us forth in His greater glory... and **I promise it will be GLORIOUS!!**

We see that the Lord had always planned from the very beginning that Job would receive the double portion of the new blessings of the **"Treasures of Darkness" AND a precious NEW REVELATION of Who God was.** It is possible that perhaps God needed Job to become twice as humble as he was before and then he would really be able to see God as SO much bigger than he saw Him before! God was definitely enlarging Job's character so He could bless him with twice as much as he had in the beginning! We can see how Job came to the very end of himself when he said in Job 13:15 "Though he slay me; yet will I trust Him."

This particular Scripture changed my life forever!

That was a huge crossroads in my own journey! It was one of the darkest times in my life! I know exactly when that happened to me, I know precisely where I was and the day and the time! I remember speaking that particular Scripture out aloud as my tears rolled down my face and meaning it with all my heart and soul because I suddenly truly saw how far from the likeness of Christ my life still was! Oh, I loved Jesus with all my heart, but the Holy Spirit allowed me to see just a tiny glimpse of myself in the light of His holiness. I had been repenting for several weeks of everything I could think of but... on that day I came to the end of myself! That was when The Spirit actually spoke to me saying, "Gill you are a million times worse than you think you are... and I LOVE YOU and I ALWAYS WILL LOVE YOU!

These are treasures that you will never forget!

So, what happened to Job? Yes, he completely humbled himself as he saw himself in the light of God's awesome majesty! Let's read Job 42:3-6 The Lord said to Job... "Who is this that darkens and obscures counsel by words without knowledge?" **Job responded...** "Therefore I now see I have rashly uttered what I did not understand, things too wonderful for me, which I did not know... I have heard of you only by the hearing of the ear, **but now my spiritual eyes see you.** Therefore I loathe myself and repent in dust and ashes". ... As a result, the Lord turned the captivity of Job and restored his fortunes when **he prayed for his friends**.

As Job turned in repentance...
The Lord gave him twice as much as he had before!

Finally, we read that Job had a great party with his friends and family who came to sympathize with him because of all the trials and calamities that had happened to him. Every man gave him a piece of money, and every man gave Job an earring of gold. And the Lord blessed the latter days of Job more than his beginning; for he had 14,000 sheep, 6,000camels, 1,000 yoke of oxen and 1,000 female donkeys. He also had seven sons and three daughters. There were no women, in all the land as beautiful as the daughters of Job, and their father gave them inheritance among their brothers.

Job was surely blessed with double treasures out of the trials he endured!

When darkness strikes or things happen, most of us are totally unaware of our own failings or short comings... yes, we can be just like Job!! But the truth is that God has a plan and He is preparing us so that we can **"Receive the Treasures of Darkness"** that we could hardly imagine in our wildest dreams!! The Lord in His immense goodness and loving kindness will grace us to keep focused on the treasures and not the darkness! So that we can come out into His marvellous light with at least twice the blessings we ever had before and a TESTIMONY that gives all the glory to the Father... Hallelujah!

Conclusion

God does His very best work in Darkness!

The Lord says to you... "Fear not for I am with you!"

I pray for you oh my dearest reader, as you have read this book that something deep inside you has been eternally stirred to seek and keep on seeking these God-given treasures. You will need courage and commitment and the help of the Holy Spirit Himself. If you are in earnest and really hungry for more of the Lord, then His anointing will be upon you and His grace will carry you through. Then you will find that the Lord, Himself will open the Scriptures to you and you will see wonderful things in His Word that will transform you from glory to Glory!

You are the Lord's own special treasure!

The Cross is the gateway to all the most incredible treasures you could ever imagine, and they are stored up for you! May be you remember how Joseph opened up all the storehouses in Egypt when he was raised up as ruler... **BUT NOW Jesus Christ has opened up ALL the storehouses of Heaven to us**... He did it when He was raised up from the dead and ascended into Heaven! Resurrection treasures abound to us as Jesus rules in all His Majesty and Glory, enthroned above and He is just waiting to share His inheritance with you and me! **WOW! WOW! WOW!**

We are seated with Christ in the Heavenly Realm!

"The Lord bless you and watch over you, guard you and keep you;
The Lord make His face to shine upon you and enlighten you and be
gracious, kind, merciful, and giving favour to you; The Lord lift up His
approving countenance upon you and give you peace, tranquillity of heart
and life continually." Numbers 6:24-26

"DARE to RECEIVE the TREASURES of DARKNESS"

Dare to Receive the Treasures of Darkness

PRAYER of SALVATION ... It would be great if you say this out loud!

Father in Heaven I acknowledge that I am a sinner and that I have fallen short of your perfect standards and I have gone my own way. I deserve to be judged for all my sins. Thank You for not leaving me in this mess, for I believe you sent Jesus Christ your only Begotten Son, who was born of a virgin and that He died for me and took all my punishment on the CROSS. I believe Jesus was raised up from the dead on the third day and He is now seated at your right hand as My Lord and Saviour. So, on this day .... I surrender my life entirely to the Lordship of Jesus Christ. I believe that Jesus is the Son of God. So, Lord Jesus I choose to confess you as my Lord and Saviour. Please come into my heart through the Holy Spirit and change me into a child of God. I renounce the things of darkness and please forgive all my sins. Please wash me with the blood of your Son Jesus Christ and make me a New Creation. From this day forward I will no longer live to please myself but live to please you who died to give me the free gift of Eternal Life. I thank you Lord Jesus for loving me so much and I now give my life completely in your hands. I receive by faith, a new heart and a right spirit within me as I put my trust in you and receive your loving mercy to me. Thank you, again, dear Lord Jesus Christ for being my Saviour. Amen.

PRAYER to be FILLED with the HOLY SPIRIT...

Father God, in the Name of Jesus Christ, I come to you humbly as your child to receive your promised Holy Spirit! You said in your Word, "If anyone asked for the Holy Spirit, you would not give them a stone!" I believe you are a good, good Father, so with joy, expectation and gratitude for all you have done on the Cross for me... I dare to ask you! Please will you baptise me in the Holy Spirit and with fire according to your Word? I need you to empower me to serve you with all my heart. I receive all you have for me... I surrender all that I am and all that I have to you my Lord. You promised in your word to give me ability and power when the Holy Spirit comes upon me, including the release of the Gift of Tongues as a love language to speak to you. So now in faith, I receive and welcome you my God the Holy Spirit so that I can speak in new tongues to glorify your name. I breathe you into my innermost being. Overflow to me Lord, so that I may pour out to others and serve you and your Kingdom. I declare my love to you my master and my Lord for ever and forever! Amen.